PEACE OPERATIONS:
Developing an American Strategy

PEACE OPERATIONS:
Developing
an American Strategy

Edited by
Antonia Handler Chayes
and
George T. Raach

National Defense University Press
Washington, DC

National Defense University Press Publications

To increase general knowledge and inform discussion, the Institute for National Strategic Studies, through its publication arm the NDU Press, publishes *Strategic Forums*; McNair Papers; proceedings of University- and Institute-sponsored symposia; books relating to U.S. national security, especially to issues of joint, combined, or coalition warfare, peacekeeping operations, and national strategy; and a variety of other works designed to circulate contemporary comment and offer alternatives to current policy. The Press occasionally publishes out-of-print defense classics, historical works, and other especially timely or distinguished writing on national security.

NDU Press publications are sold by the U.S. Government Printing Office. For ordering information, call (202) 512-1800 or write to the Superintendent of Documents, U.S. Government Printing Office, Washington, DC 20402.

Library of Congress Cataloging-in-Publication Data
Peace operations : developing an American strategy / Antonia Handler Chayes and George T. Raach.
     p.   cm.
     Includes bibliographical references (p.).
     1. United States—Military policy. 2. Military assistance, American.
3. International police. I. Chayes, Antonia Handler, 1929- . II. Raach, George T., 1945- .
UA23.P377   1995
341.5'84—dc20   95-38994
                                 CIP

First Printing, October 1995

For sale by the U.S. Government Printing Office
Superintendent of Documents, Mail Stop: SSOP, Washington, DC 20402-9328
ISBN 0-16-051681-1

CONTENTS

Foreword . . . . *ix*

1. *Beyond Fighting And Winning* 3
   Antonia Handler Chayes and George T. Raach
2. *The Environment and Tasks of*
   Peace Operations 23
   William J. Durch and J. Matthew Vaccaro
3. *Lessons of the Past: Experiences in*
   Peace Operations 39
   Christine Cervanek
4. *Peace Operations and Combat Readiness* 67
   J. Matthew Vaccaro
5. *Military Perspectives on Peace Operations* 83
   George T. Raach
6. *Military Culture and Institutional Change* 103
   A. J. Bacevich
7. *Peace Operations, Emergency Law Enforcement,*
   and Constabulary Forces 115
   William Rosenau
8. *Contracting and Privatization in*
   Peace Operations 137
   Christine Cervanek and George T. Raach
9. *Coalition Management in Peace Operations* 153
   Antonia Handler Chayes and Wendy Jordan

Appendix: Protocol for Peace Operations Case Studies . . 171
About the Editors 177

FOREWORD

In 1994 Congress chartered a Commission on the Roles and Missions of the Armed Forces to examine whether the existing roles and missions were adequate to meet the challenges of the post-Cold War era. After a year of study, the Commission delivered a comprehensive report in June 1995. Among the findings, it concluded that military forces should be prepared to do more than their traditional missions of deterrence and warfighting. The Commission determined that the military can and should play a larger role in crisis management and conflict prevention, more commonly known as peace operations.

This book, which presents the most salient papers prepared for the Commission on this topic, is a step toward that strategy. What is needed, according to the authors, is an overall American strategy for peace operations. The unifying theme is that peace operations are investments in stability—dealing effectively with "precursor" instabilities may avoid the need for more substantial forces and larger investments later. The opening chapter, for example, makes the case for raising the priority of peace operations, funding them in ways that do not undermine readiness, and integrating them into planning and training for regional contingencies. The subsequent papers address related issues.

This innovative, thought-provoking volume provides military planners and decisionmakers with options to improve the effectiveness of peace operations forces. Such options are important, because it is nearly always less costly to prevent a war than to fight one. And preventing wars should always be the first recourse of diplomats and warriors.

ERVIN J. ROKKE
Lieutenant General, U.S. Air Force
President, National Defense University

PEACE OPERATIONS
Developing an American Strategy

1. BEYOND FIGHTING AND WINNING

Antonia Handler Chayes and George T. Raach

Introduction

The transition to a post-Cold War security environment has not been smooth, nor has the predicted and hoped-for degree of stability been achieved. The only apparent certainty is uncertainty and its direction is very difficult to forecast. This poses an enormous challenge to the U.S. military forces. When the most serious threat was war with the Soviet Union, we could focus almost exclusively on deterring—and if necessary, fighting and winning—that conflict. Now, U.S. security policy and strategies must be fundamentally reexamined in order to develop forces and methods of operations that can cope with multidimensional challenges that go far beyond conventional warfare. The U.S. Commission on Roles and Missions of the Armed Forces (CORM) has been part of that rethinking process, along with the entire Department of Defense—the Secretary, the Joint Chiefs of Staff, the services, and the CINCs. Given the interest of the United States in the stability of the post-Cold War world, the process logically begins with some informed estimates about future demands on the military.

Dr. Antonia Chayes was a Commissioner on the CORM. She is a former Under Secretary of the Air Force and is currently the Co-Director of the Project on International Compliance and Dispute Resolution, Program on Negotiation, Harvard Law School. Dr. Chayes is the author of numerous books and articles.

George T. Raach, a retired Army officer, is a member of the CORM's professional staff. He has been the Military Assistant to the Deputy Under Secretary of Defense for Policy, the staff director for the DOD report to Congress on the Persian Gulf War, and a member of the faculties at the Army, Navy, and National War Colleges.

The Gulf War is seen by some as a compass that points to the directions U.S. Armed Forces ought to take to prepare for their roles in future crises. Yet, with that exception, the period since 1989 has been marked by a series of lesser regional crises, ethnonational conflicts, and government breakdown side by side with some hopeful, if lumpy, post-Communist transitions. Aside from the Gulf crisis, none of these conflicts has represented immediate threats to U.S. interests, and their scale, when compared to the magnitude of the former Soviet threat, is small indeed. Nevertheless, putting aside future risks of an emerging peer competitor or regional hegemon and the proliferation of weapons of mass destruction, there is likely to be some ongoing requirement for American intervention in smaller crises. Indeed, it has already arisen, and many senior military leaders interviewed during our analysis thought it far more likely that forces would be committed for peace operations than for regional conflicts in the next decade.

For example, since 1991 there have been a number of both cross-border and internal conflicts in which U.S. forces have been engaged in peace operations of one form or another. These include humanitarian interventions in Northern Iraq, Somalia, and Rwanda; enforcement of no-fly zones in Iraq and the Former Yugoslavia; preventive force deployments to Korea and Kuwait; and operations aimed at restoring the Government of Haiti. In addition, there have been numerous instances in which United States military forces provided support to other nations engaged in peace operations, including, for example, airlifting the forces of those engaged in some areas of the Commonwealth of Independent States. A variety of motives prompted the use of American military assets in these destabilizing conflicts. Although none of these crises represented a major security threat to the United States, they did affect interests that policy makers believed required American military response. In almost all cases the common thread seems to be the belief that the judicious use of the U.S. military could help to cope with incipient conflicts that, left untended, might well involve substantial commitments later.

These examples do not necessarily serve as forecasts, of course, and the United States ought not to be engaged in all areas where conflict arises. As part of developing a new strategy, tt is important to identify conflict situations that might be mitigated by peace operations, especially in areas important enough to U.S. interests that civilian decisionmakers would probably commit forces if a regional conflict were to erupt (*inter alia* in NATO countries, in the vicinity of NATO, the Middle East, Southwest Asia, Korea, and Central America in some cases.) There is a clear and significant national interest in maintaining international stability in such areas by limiting or containing violence and its human consequences, and that interest often can only be furthered by the use of the military .

Policy statements by both Republican and Democratic administrations emphasize the importance of peace operations in reducing instability and limiting conflict. While it is clear that military force cannot solve the underlying problems that cause instability, it may create space for diplomatic and economic efforts to prevent or resolve conflict. Some situations might compel America to exercise leadership to lead or participate in peace operations, even at considerable risk and cost, because significant U.S. interests are at stake. Should an agreement be reached in the Balkans, should a comprehensive Middle East peace depend upon it, should Cuba dissolve into chaos, or Macedonia erupt into a spillover war involving Greece and Turkey, the United States might decide that its interests required substantial commitment of forces. In such instances and within established parameters, peace operations can be seen as efforts to forestall larger regional conflicts.

However, decisionmakers should realize that even with rational models and established parameters, situations will arise that may compel the United States to participate in peace operations. Humanitarian issues may seem compelling; domestic political pressures and pressures from allies may develop; and a range of foreign and domestic policy issues may require response, even if important U.S. security interests are not at stake directly.

Military strategists and planners should be aware, also, that in a democratic society and an interdependent world, sometimes decisions will be made outside established parameters for interventions. That makes the development of a strategy and the establishment of criteria all the more important, although planning for such events is necessarily less predictable and necessarily of lower priority. The systematic ability to analyze both the significance for national security and the immediate rationale for involvement may permit policy makers to withstand pressures if the consequences might be negative, or set limits that reduce potential harm.

The ongoing debate over the past several years about U.S. involvement in the former Yugoslavia is a microcosm of the varied and conflicting pressures that may arise. Some combination of assessment of national interest weighed against risk has militated against any commitment of ground troops while hostilities continue. Yet the importance of protecting allies may cause the policy to bend somewhat before the war ends, and the United States may become involved in an operation on a scale that may have been unnecessary if a strategy and the organization of national assets to support it had been available to prevent the crisis in the first place.

Traditionally, peace operations, especially peacekeeping, were viewed as operations that came at the tail end of conflict (as discussed in chapter 2). There will continue to be a need for peace operations to assist in bringing about and guaranteeing peace. However, the value of peace operations in dealing with precursor instabilities--to prevent, contain, or ameliorate incipient conflicts-- must be considered also. In this sense, peace operations are investments. Properly conducted by forces that have planned, prepared and trained for them within the proper strategic framework, peace operations may well preclude the need to deploy larger forces at substantial costs in both blood and treasure later.

Thus, while DOD is currently planning for two nearly simultaneous major regional conflicts (MRCs) similar to the Gulf

War, it would appear that the American military will be called upon to use its skills in a greater variety of conflict and conflict prevention operations. The likelihood of the use of force in scenarios beyond conventional conflict has several implications. During the Cold War, a case could be made that, by preparing for war with the Soviets, the United States created forces trained and equipped to deal with lesser included crises. There is some validity to this argument because the lesser crises scripted by planners during the Cold War period resembled the sort of conventional conflict we envisioned with the Soviet Union (e.g., a war in Korea would be a smaller version of a war on Europe's central front.) Therefore, the same sorts of forces, organized, trained and equipped in the same way, would be adequate for both. However, in the current period, there is less similarity between the requirements of MRCs that might occur in the Middle East and Korea and the tasks required by peace operations.

This does not suggest that different or specialized forces are required to cope with each type of operation or that a separate set of programs is necessary. Rather, the implication is that, while the primary function of the American military continues to be winning wars, it must understand and prepare for the full range of potential interventions, not just those that involve conventional "fight and win" combat. The full values of a flexible, robust force capable of dealing with the range of ambiguous conflicts that may require a response is not yet realized. Fighting and winning wars are quite properly the *primary* functions of the military, but there is a danger if it is perceived to be the *only* function. A concept in which forces can only fight and win conflicts is inadequate. Although some conflicts may be deterred thereby, others are not prevented, contained, or mitigated. A larger strategic tapestry demands a full range of military options to deal with precursors to regional conflicts.

Arriving at conclusions that facilitate this new understanding of the ways that military force can be used was an important element in the work of the CORM. Once the reality is accepted that the United States, if it is to maintain its leadership, will somehow be required to be involved in peace operations, policy makers in the Executive Branch and Congress may be able to address ways in which such involvement can be more strategically effective (in terms of furthering national interests without unduly taxing the armed forces) and more efficient (in terms of prudent expenditures of funds and other resources). This book is devoted to issues raised for the United States by the requirements of post-Cold War peace operations. The CORM was concerned with:

- The priority afforded peace operations by planners and programmers
- The tasks encompassed by the term "peace operations"
- Which departments, agencies and nongovernmental entities are best suited for performing these tasks
- How such tasks impact traditional military operations and military culture
- The training required to perform them
- The importance of such tasks to national and international security.

In sum, we looked at two general questions:

- How should peace operations be integrated in operational planning and training regimes?
- Should there be changes in current DOD organization and budgeting for peace operations?

A Matter of Priority

The strategic relationship of peace operations to the preparation for and conduct of war is often both oversimplified and misunderstood. The typology of peace operations discussed in the next chapter encompasses classic or traditional peacekeeping, second generation or multidimensional peacekeeping, humanitarian interventions, and peace enforcement. That chapter also lists some of the tasks associated with these operations. Understanding these factors is important; however, it is equally necessary to understand the relationship between peace operations and preparations for lesser regional conflicts (LRCs) and MRCs. The CORM concluded that peace operations are more closely related to regional conflict than is generally acknowledged now. Although an increasing number of military leaders and strategists do understand the relevance of peace operations to national security, there are those who continue to view them as detracting from the military's primary function of fighting and winning wars. For the most part, those who view peace operations as a detractor see them as something entirely different from, and only remotely associated with, conventional military operations. In taking this view, they overlook the value of peace operations as a measure to fill a gap between the sorts of activities conducted during periods of relative peace and the outbreak of large-scale hostilities. This is a sort of bipolar view of the scale of options. In essence, what it suggests is that there is deterrence on one end of the spectrum and war on the other, and there is little between the two worthy of note.

One effect of this perspective is that some military planners do not give a very high priority to peace operations, despite their preventive value. The military uses a typology to categorize operations and assign priorities to them which reflects this view. From the military perspective, operations fall into two main divisions: combat operations associated with deterring or fighting MRCs, and Operations Other Than War (OOTW). For the military, the former has a much higher priority, even though MRCs are much less likely than other operations.

OOTW is not a useful category for analysis. Civilian policy makers and military planners need greater refinement of category. In a world so fraught with conflict, in which U.S. involvement is so widely sought, they must be able to establish priorities and distinguish among conflict situations on the basis of sound and justifiable criteria. They must be able to gauge the importance of involvement for preventing a larger and messier conflict on the scale of an MRC. In that context, analysis for informed decisions should focus on the type of mission and on the potential for achieving operational objectives with acceptable force levels at minimal risk. OOTW blurs conflict distinctions.

Missions consigned to OOTW are "ghettoized" and somewhat indistinct. Peace operations are currently one of more than a dozen OOTW. Accordingly, as is the case with other missions in this category, they are given a low priority for programming, planning, and training—until the military is called upon to intervene in a crisis. Thus, although the military has responded immediately to policy decisions to participate in peace operations, many military leaders continue to regard such operations as a diversion and outside their planned activities. Consequently, when the President decides to deploy forces to a peace operation, ad hoc measures are often taken to cobble together an operation of available—but not necessarily properly trained or equipped—forces funded from existing budgets at some cost to the rest of the force.

Some have argued that no peace operation has failed because of a lack of properly trained forces. That conclusion is questionable, but even if accepted at face value, it does not mean that better preparation (in terms of training, equipment, organization, and funding) will not improve the effectiveness of U.S. forces in peace operations. Nor does it mean that national policy objectives cannot be achieved more completely and at lower cost with better preparation. However, for effectiveness to improve, the priority of peace operations as a valuable strategic asset must increase, and all other options turn on that improvement.

One way of raising the priority, of course, is to elevate peace operations from a collateral to a primary or common function for the Armed Forces. Functions in these categories are delineated in Department of Defense Directive 5100.1 (*Functions of the Department of Defense and Its Major Components*) and may be used as sole justification for force structure and procurement. For example, ground combat is a common function of both the Army and the Marine Corps and both use that justification to design forces and develop and procure equipment. Designating peace operations as a primary function for one service or a common function for several services would raise the priority, but it is a somewhat drastic step that, at present, is unnecessary because there are other remedies.

Another option is to adopt a strategy that removes those peace operations designed to prevent or mitigate precursor instabilities from OOTW and establishes them as a distinct category of operation conducted in pursuit of important national interests as outlined above, and given resources accordingly. This can be accomplished through planning directives and changes to doctrine that align and integrate peace operations with plans to cope with conventional regional conflicts. As war plans are drafted by the Joint Staff and the Unified Combatant Commands, opportunities to use forces in peace operations to prevent, contain, or ameliorate crises in their early stages would be systematically examined, and requirements for service capabilities determined. The services, in turn, would program as necessary for procurement and training and, when contingencies arise, provide the Unified Commanders with sufficiently large, combat-ready forces organized, trained, and equipped to satisfy their requirements. Units told to prepare for peace operations by the Services would give appropriate priority to training for those skills required by peace operations. All this would occur not ad hoc but as part of deliberate planning regimes. As a result of a higher priority, forces would be better prepared to engage in peace operations without sacrificing capability to conduct other operations and with a better chance of precluding conflict.

An implication of this action is greater integration of training and preparation for peace operations into the overall training and preparation regimes. For units likely to be involved in peace operations, this will require a reevaluation of mission essential task lists (METLs) to identify current tasks that require some specialized training for peace operations and to include tasks that may be new. Training programs to achieve the new standards required by METL reviews must be flexible and expansive, perhaps along the lines of the program at the Joint Readiness Training Center at Fort Polk, LA. This program permits units that are likely to be involved in peace operations to train in a scenario that emphasizes the skills required by these operations, as well as conventional warfighting skills should peace operations prove unsuccessful or should they be required to confront conventional warfighting crises at another time. Other training programs that may be adapted for peace operations training include those used by the Special Forces to train personnel across a broad range of tasks.

The first issue that must be resolved to develop a new strategy and improve effectiveness, however, is assigning peace operations a priority consistent with their potential to avert conflict in some situations is. While simply improving the priority will do much to improve training and integration of peace operations with preparations for MRCs, it is not the only issue. There are concerns about readiness and how to organize resources for these operations as well.

Readiness

The debate about whether or not peace operations degrade readiness has become highly politicized and almost theological. So long as peace operations are considered to be OOTW, the mindset will be that preparation for and engagement in them detract from true military readiness.

But readiness is not a matter of mindset alone. There are serious practical issues. The first of these involves funding of peace operations. Perhaps more than any other factor, the diversion of funds that occurs to pay for peace operations has the largest impact on readiness. Despite repeated involvement in peace operations since the end of the Cold War, advance funding has not been provided. Therefore, in order to offset contingency costs, the Services must draw upon the Operations and

Maintenance Accounts (OMA) of units that are not deployed. This, in turn, means that bill-paying units will have to curtail training, defer maintenance or replenishment of supply stocks, or take some other action that will likely undermine short- and perhaps long-term readiness. If reimbursement is delayed too long, the effects of the initial shifts cascade as opportunity costs mount. Thus, so long as the Department tries to fund peace operations "out of hide," it will be able to do neither peace operations nor preparations for conventional warfighting well. The fact that OMA funds are likely to be taken from units that are among the last to be deployed to battle mitigates this "borrowing" only a little.

The lack of advance funding and/or timely reimbursement once operations are underway is key to readiness degradation. American forces have performed well in peace operations thus far, but often at a real cost. The costs are substantial because OMA have almost no margin for contingencies. Reimbursements for funds diverted from OMA either are partial, lag badly, or both. The Executive Branch and Congress must make the decision to enter into peace operations, not sidle into them, understand the costs, and pay them. No war or regional conflict is taken out of hide. The services and the CINCs should not be required to curtail training and maintenance activities because OMA must be used to pay for actual peace operations.

Fortunately, no one argues that the process for funding is working; further, there is general recognition that improvements must be made. However, the methods by which funding can be made more effective remain highly contentious political issues between the Executive Branch and Congress. These methods include, *inter alia*, first, more rigorous use of current procedures to ensure timely reimbursement through supplemental appropriations. A second option is for DOD to develop and submit to Congress advanced estimates of costs based on historical data. These estimates would be periodically updated by the Department, and Congress would act on associated requests for reimbursement using a fast-track approach.

Third, along the lines of the proposal submitted this year with the DOD budget, Congress could authorize the Department to incur unfunded obligations under carefully specified circumstances to pay for peace operations without depleting OMA first. Although Congress declined to approve this measure during their deliberations over the Fiscal Year 1996 budget, the concept has merit and should not be abandoned outright. Establishing a "line of credit" and providing estimates of costs require careful thinking through the strategic equation at the outset (which has the advantage of precluding inadvertent "mission creep") and examining goals, objectives, and measures of success at critical points during the operation. There is positive merit in such processes.

Any of these, and a number of other options as well, would do much to avoid adversely effecting readiness by curtailing training and maintenance. Of course, numerous points of tension exist between the Congress, which is reluctant to give the Executive Branch too much leeway, and the ExecutiveBranch, which is often leery of Congressional meddling with what it sees as its foreign policy prerogatives. Also, the political debate concerning these options is obscured somewhat by the fact that cost data for peace operations have not been transparent, and accounting methods are not consistent throughout DOD. Presumably, this will improve as recent experiences are analyzed; officials of both the Department and the Office of Management and Budget informed the CORM staff that current accounting practices are much more efficient as a result of these experiences. Improved accountability would not cure political differences but would permit Congress to perform its oversight function more effectively and avoid delays in reimbursements that result from incomplete information. But whatever the course of action, ensuring that funds are available promptly to reimburse the costs of peace operations is a critical step in developing an overall strategy. Because strategies serve as a bridge between objectives and the resources available to accomplish those objectives, it is important that planners can be assured resources will be available.

A second argument presented concerning readiness is that peace operations divert organizational focus and resources from preparing for warfighting. This argument needs to be unpacked and analyzed. It is true that peace operations may impact the immediate readiness of units to perform specific tasks, if the same forces are used immediately for entirely different missions in a different operational environment. For example, some troops involved in maintaining civil order in Haiti would require proficiency training in some combat skills prior to deployment for a conventional war in Korea. Yet an analysis done by the 10th Mountain Division indicates many factors determining force readiness were either improved or fully maintained by the experience in Haiti, with only one showing degradation over normal training routines. Therefore, peace operations appear to offer some opportunities that go beyond what is available in garrison, or even at major training centers, and this applies across a broad range of units and skills.

A third facet of readiness concerns involves personnel tempo or PERSTEMPO, which is a measurement of time that service members spend deployed away from their home stations. PERSTEMPO is excessive for some forces that have been engaged repeatedly in peace operations; this excess, which occurs for several reasons, can have a deleterious long-term effect on readiness by undermining retention. As noted, the current low priority of peace operations has hampered planning, and each situation uses ad hoc planning. As a result, training adjustments are not made systematically, even though Services know that some tasks are unique to peace operations and require either specialized training or equipment, planning, and programming in advance of operations. These requirements reinforce the use of the most experienced forces over and over, eroding their morale and even affecting military retention because the quality of life has deteriorated. As was true of funding, improving the priority of peace operations will likely have a positive influence on PERSTEMPO rates as planners recognize that peace operations will continue to demand the performance of the American military in a variety of situations and allocate resources over a broader base of forces.

Broadening the Base

Peace operations involve a large range of tasks and activities. It is our contention that they could be performed more effectively with less strain on resources, readiness, and morale. At present, a limited number of Active Component (AC) forces are asked to perform many of these tasks in the first instance because a potentially hostile operational environment makes it inadvisable to use nonmilitary resources, military skills are called for, or a rapid response is required. Yet sometimes the AC military is called upon simply because it is the most available and politically feasible organization, given the current low priority for peace operations, not because of a requirement for its specialized skills.

There is ample experience now to identify tasks and environments that require AC military presence. Conversely, enough is known to identify areas and environments where other resources could be used in far greater measure than they have been thus far. An effort to identify tasks and assign responsibilities ought to be undertaken as part of the process to develop a stratetic concept of peace operations in order to distribute the work load more equitably for peace operations. As a guide, the activities assigned to the military—both AC and Reserve Components (RC)—should conform to their core competencies and avoid functions that the military could perform, but for which realistic alternatives exist outside DOD. (Making this assessment assures identification of those conditions under which the military might be called upon to undertake responsibility for essentially nonmilitary functions.)

A good start would be to inventory tasks that peace operations have thus far entailed and carefully assess the capabilities of other U.S. Government departments and agencies, industrial contractors, nongovernmental organizations and other nations to perform them, perhaps under the auspices of a

Presidential Review Directive. Part of this assessment has to be political feasibility. No strategy will work if civilian agencies, not budgeted for peace operations, are called upon to perform tasks, or if contractors go unpaid. Once the assessment is complete, it is possible to develop an overall plan for using alternatives to AC and RC military forces where that seems feasible and prudent, and to develop a strategy of assistance for non-DOD actors where needed to improve the necessary capabilities.

Reserve Components

As noted, peace operations currently use a disproportionate share of AC units. Perhaps because of the low priority and lack of a coherent strategy for these operations, RC units have rarely been involuntarily called up to support peace operations, although numerous RC volunteers have participated. The RC clearly possess many capabilities required for peace operations, especially air crews, civil affairs, military police, engineering, and logistics units. But when these capabilities cannot be made available through significant numbers of volunteers or selected callup, the few AC units with similar capabilities are used repeatedly, contributing among other things to the PERSTEMPO problem. For example, 70 percent of the 10th Mountain Division, an AC unit, has been continuously deployed for than 2 years. Many other forces have also been deployed for long periods.

There are no structural barriers to mobilizing RC units to assist directly in peace operations or "back fill" AC units involved in those operations for MRC-related tasks. Thus, in more closely integrating peace operations with planning for regional conflicts, portions of the RC should be mobilized for all but the smallest and briefest operations and included as part of peace operations planning as a matter of course. While repeated activation of RC forces can be deleterious to the readiness of that component, especially if adequate reimbursement is not forthcoming, sufficient numbers of RC units exist so that involuntary mobilization could be spread over a fairly broad base, thus avoiding repetitive mobilizations.

Length of mobilization can be a problem, but not an insurmountable one. In the case of some tasks (e.g., logistics support of U.S. forces), RC rotations into the area of operations could take the place of the usual annual training period. However, where requirements dictate, RC commitments in peace operations may extend beyond these limits. For example, MP units that interact with the local population need time to learn their "beat." To be effective contributors, units of this sort should be mobilized and deployed for several months. If requirements of this sort are laid out by planners well in advance by according peace operations a higher priority, the impact on participating units can be minimized beyond what occurs with *ad hoc* spur-of-the-moment mobilizations. An example of the success of this approach is found in the current 6-month deployment of a predominantly RC force to the Sinai-based Multinational Force and Observers which oversees the Camp David Accords. After all, participation in peace operations does have considerable training value for RC forces. Thus, involving the RC to a greater extent reduces the impact on AC forces by expanding the pool of available units, and it improves the effectiveness of units involved in peace operations by reducing organizational fatigue while improving the readiness of participating RC units.

Nonmilitary Resources and Organizations

Although military forces will always perform a significant amount of the tasks in peace operations, they are by no means the only resources available to the Government in high-priority situations. Nonmilitary assets include other government departments and agencies, commercial contractors, and other nations and international organizations. In recent peace operations, military forces have operated airfields, supported the training of indigenous constabulary forces, provided physical security in benign environments, restored and operated parts of the civilian infrastructure, distributed food and relief supplies directly to deprived populations, and provided medical care to those populations. Each of these functions required the expenditure of military resources; each could have been accomplished by nonmilitary entities.

The integration of non-DOD organziations in peace operations should be given careful consideration in the development of peace operations strategies. As the case studies illustrate, peace operations are dynamic, and it is often not possible to determine the tasks that will require military capabilities dictated by the environment in advance. But these studies also highlight the fact that environments are often benign enough to allow nonmilitary resources to replace the military assets that were initially deployed. Other agencies of the government could make a significant contribution in these circumstances, and should do so. Part of the process for institutionalizing the participation by these organizations should be built on the high-level interagency review of tasks and responsibilities mentioned in the previous section. Such a review should include the Department of Justice, the Department of State, and the U.S. Agency for International Development and may be extended to include nongovernmental organizations such as the International Red Cross. It would be most useful if the process of review were to produce a Presidential Decision Directive that would authoritatively assign responsibilities to government departments and organizations and identify those responsibilities the government would leave for private organizations.

Commercial contracting constitutes a second category of nonmilitary contribution. Contractors can fulfill a number of requirements including law enforcement and constabulary force training, as well as more traditional tasks such as logistics support of deployed forces or base construction. Contracting is not an unmixed blessing, however. It is difficult to engage contractors if funding is uncertain, for example, and will be until that mechanism is repaired. Then, too, the contracting process can be lengthy and unresponsive to the sorts of changes that case studies of peace operations indicate will occur. Finally, it is important for decisionmakers to understand the amount of control required with respect to certain functions and activities. In many cases, that requirement will be minimal and lack of close government control of activities will not have much impact on the operation as a whole. In other cases, the means used to accomplish the task have great importance because contracting generally means the loss of some control over how the contractor accomplishes the requirements of the contract.

The assets of other nations and international organizations. are resources that will relieve some of the burden on the U.S. military and may, given the proper impetus, improve the effectiveness of peace operations. The Departments of State and Defense should take inventory of the skills and assets of international organizations and individual states. Some requirements for peace operations will have to be provided by the U.S. military—for example, substantial strategic lift and a logistics system capable of sustaining large numbers of forces over long distances for extended periods of time. There are other areas, however, where the United States by no means has a monopoly.

In most peace operations, for example, a need exists for substantial numbers of military police and light infantry. The United States certainly has these types of units, but so do many other nations, and they should be encouraged to provide them. In some cases, the United States might be required to offer some additional training and guidance or operational assistance to units provided by other nations. However, over time and with minimum expense and effort, the Department might create a pool of capable forces in other states that could relieve the U.S. military of part of the operational burden in return for support in areas where the United States has unique expertise.

In essence, then, effectiveness in peace operations can be enhanced by expanding the resource base for such operations beyond the military. Such an expansion permits the military to conserve assets that may be needed for conventional operations and enhances the nation's ability to undertake peace operations that might well prevent larger crises. For the most part, expanding the base does not appreciably increase the operational costs in the long run. For example, contracting involves additional costs, but that alternative may be less expensive than relying on military resources. Broadening the base also takes advantage of the special talents and skills that others bring to the mission; simply because the military can accomplish a task does not mean that it is the best suited to do so. If decisionmakers elect to participate in peace operations, that participation should be predicated on a serious effort that takes advantage of all available capabilities in a synergistic way.

Conclusion

Developing an American strategy for peace operations requires an assessment of the objectives of these operations and methods available to improve the resources needed to accomplish those objectives. Broadly, peace operations contribute to the national strategic objectives that enhance stability in regions critical to the United States by dealing with precursor instabilities and containing and ameliorating conflict in ways that may preclude requirements for larger forces later. Providing definitive form to this strategy of prevention requires adequate resources, to permit effective operations at acceptable cost.

The measures described in this chapter and expanded upon throughout this volume can do a great deal to improve the effectiveness and efficiency in the conduct of peace operations, while alleviating undue burdens on American forces. Assigning peace operations a priority commensurate with their value in preventing conflict, aligning them with planning for regional conflict, and allowing limited funding for training and equipment will help realize the full potential of peace operations as a conflict management tool.

Insuring that services do not have to forego training and needed maintenance in order to fund peace operations eliminates a major force readiness problem. Serious treatment of funding discrepancies will also have a positive effect on morale in these units because service members will be able to train to an acceptable level in an uncurtailed fashion using fully operational equipment. Advanced funding may not be feasible, but prompt and complete reimbursement will help minimize the problem.

Sorting out responsibilities, integrating Active and Reserve forces more closely in peace operations, and ensuring involvement by other departments, agencies, and organizations will help to reduce operating and personnel tempo irritants. So will outsourcing appropriate activities. And, where feasible to do so, the United States should draw upon the capabilities of other nations to supplement its own, even when doing so requires an investment in the preparation of those nations' forces.

Unless the world changes drastically—or the United States withdraws from it—there will be occasions where containment and prevention of conflict through peace operations will appear the best policy option. When a decision to use American forces for that purpose arises, they must be ready in just as professional a manner as they are to engage in conventional combat, or the policy cannot succeed. And what is needed now is a larger repertoire of policy options, not more limited ones, to ease the difficult and complex transitions from the Cold War. We remain confident that the military is able and willing to respond to that requirement and will not remain mired in the past.

2. THE ENVIRONMENT AND TASKS OF PEACE OPERATIONS

William J. Durch and J. Matthew Vaccaro

Recent experience of the U.S. Armed Forces demonstrates that general purpose forces can accomplish peace operations adequately. For instance, the U.S.-led unified task force (UNITAF) in Somalia achieved its objective of ensuring a secure environment for the delivery of humanitarian assistance. Likewise, the U.S. forces engaged in Haiti have made steady progress toward their goals. That U.S. forces can accomplish missions that go well beyond their primary purpose of deterrence and combat is a testament to the high-quality personnel in the Armed Forces and the embodiment of flexibility and adaptability into U.S. war-fighting doctrine. Nonetheless, experience has also shown that contemporary peace operations are different from traditional combat operations in terms of political-military environment, operational objectives and, consequently, tasks assigned to forces in the field. An understanding of these differences and their operational implications is essential to make

---

Dr. William J. Durch is a Senior Associate at the Henry L. Stimson Center in Washington, DC. He is the editor and principal author of *The Evolution of U.N. Peacekeeping*.

J. Matthew Vaccaro is a Senior Analyst at DFI International, a research and consulting firm in Washington, DC, where he manages studies on conflict resolution.

informed judgments about how the Department of Defense could package or adapt forces to conduct peace operations with greater effectiveness and safety.

The Environment and Objectives of Peace Operations

Peace operations take place, almost by definition, in a multilateral political-military environment that usually requires forces to exhibit impartiality and restraint in the use of force to an unaccustomed degree. They may find themselves positioned to implement a cease-fire between two fighting forces, or deployed in the midst of the civilian population of a country trying, with international assistance, to recover from a recent civil war. In either case, the rules of engagement may prevent siding with any local faction, and highly restrain the use of force except where required for immediate self-defense. Recourse to force may even signal the failure of the mission.

The objectives of peace operations generally will include neither victory, in the ordinary sense of defeating a defined enemy militarily, nor the identification of an enemy. The equivalent of victory is successful implementation of a mandate—maintaining the political-military status quo, for example, or facilitating implementation of a peace accord. The latter mission may entail the temporary maintenance of civic order. Peace enforcement operations deviate from these objectives in certain respects.

Whereas combat operations may involve only U.S. forces, peace operations are almost always undertaken in cooperation with other countries and increasingly under an internationally agreed-upon operational mandate. Given that most states insist on retaining ultimate command and control of the forces they contribute to such operations, command and control in peace operations tends to be hazier than in combat operations and may be subject to continual re-negotiation with home governments. Logistics and resupply are similarly complicated by the multinational character of most peace operations. Finally, varying levels of training and capability among military units make all but the simplest and most static peace operations difficult to implement and restrict the ability of an operation to adapt to changing political-military circumstances.[1] The major subcategories of peace operations include traditional peacekeeping, multidimensional peacekeeping, humanitarian intervention, and peace enforcement.[2]

Traditional Peacekeeping

A traditional peacekeeping force is by definition neutral and positioned between former belligerents. It monitors a cease-fire and creates the political space for negotiation of the dispute in question. These missions are conducted with the full consent of all parties to the conflict and most often are put into place after a cease-fire (but not necessarily an all-encompassing settlement) has been achieved, for example, after the Suez Crisis (1956), the October War (1973), or the Iran-Iraq War (1988). Use of force is authorized only for self-defense or defense of the mission, and then largely to deter small-scale threats, not the general resumption of fighting. Facing the latter threat, peacekeepers generally have been withdrawn (Sinai 1967), or have stood aside after token resistance (Lebanon 1982), although in one instance (Nicosia, Cyprus, airport 1974) U.N. units put up stiff resistance to invading forces.

Traditional peacekeeping predominated during the Cold War and served U.S. and Soviet desires to avoid a direct clash of arms in regions of tension. With the exception of the Congo operation (1960-64), these missions involved military components only. Diplomatic efforts to resolve the underlying dispute proceeded separately from peacekeeping operations, which were often of prolonged duration without a fixed schedule leading to termination.

Multidimensional Peacekeeping

This type of operation emerged near the end of the Cold War as a number of conflicts with East-West dimensions came to a close, and the permanent members of the U.N. Security Council were able to agree on more ambitious operations to help countries in transition to a sustainable peace. Multidimensional peace operations often have mandates that not only facilitate the reduction of tensions between former foes (as in traditional peacekeeping), but also help implement a peace accord that addresses the causes of the underlying conflict. In most cases, and unlike traditional peacekeeping, multidimensional operations have an implementation schedule and a timeline. When the tasks on the schedule have been completed, the operation folds its tents and departs. The existence of an operational deadline gives the United Nations and the external powers that may have influence with various local parties, more leverage than an openended mandate to induce compliance with a peace accord. However, the general political environment must be such that the worst consequences of compliance (after losing a U.N. supervised election, for example) are still preferable to taking up arms once again. Otherwise, peace may fall apart, as it did in Angola in 1992.

Because multidimensional peacekeeping primarily involves settlements of internal conflicts, it operates in a much more complex domestic political environment than traditional peacekeeping. Moreover, although a multidimensional operation is usually conducted with the full consent of the former belligerents, its military component may be authorized to use limited force against local elements that are actively hindering the activities of the peace operation. Thus, multidimensional peacekeeping can entail greater risk of hostilities than traditional operations and greater pressure to use force to keep a peace accord on track.

In contrast to traditional peacekeeping, multidimensional operations usually have sizable civilian components (which may outnumber the military component) and a U.N. civilian chief of mission (a Special Representative of the Secretary General). The civilian components may include civil administrators, election administrators and/or poll watchers, an information section to educate the public about electoral processes and help develop grass-roots democratic institutions, refugees and displaced persons resettlement units, a component to monitor and report human rights abuses, and civilian police. The military component serves in a supporting role, maintaining a secure environment in which the civilian components can work. This role may involve a number of tasks not found in traditional peacekeeping.

Humanitarian Intervention

Whereas the two previous sections describe techniques employed by the international community to secure an emerging peace, humanitarian intervention is conducted to relieve suffering in the midst of an ongoing conflict or situation of anarchy. It is considered a temporary measure to help citizens survive until a cease-fire can be reached and, possibly, multidimensional peacekeeping can begin. Humanitarian intervention may be accompanied by a parallel diplomatic initiative to reach a negotiated settlement of the conflict (as in Bosnia), or the operation's leadership may be assigned that task (as in Somalia).

The lack of a pre-existing cease-fire makes humanitarian intervention qualitatively different from peacekeeping. Such intervention may not involve the consent of all parties to the conflict and may appear to violate local sovereignty. However, a U.N. Security Council resolution that invokes a "threat to international peace and security" can overrule the U.N. Charter's otherwise blanket prohibition on intervention "in matters which are essentially within the domestic jurisdiction of any state." Such threats may include the risk of a conflict spreading to other states, or an exodus of refugees that threatens regional political stability. Humanitarian intervention may also be viewed as an effort to protect the sources of a state's sovereignty, namely, its populace, from the ravages of civil war or a renegade government. Examples of such operations would include the U.S.- and U.N.-led operations in Somalia (1992-95), the U.N. operation in Bosnia-Herzegovina (1992-), and the U.S.-led Operation *Provide Comfort* and its successors in northern Iraq (1991-).

Humanitarian intervention is a rather new type of peace operation and operationally quite difficult. "Intervention" implies an operation that may be violently opposed by one or more parties to an ongoing conflict. Although a humanitarian operation may attempt to keep its distance from all local fighting factions, local perceptions of U.N. impartiality have proven very difficult to sustain in the midst of continued fighting, particularly when the civilian population is itself considered a prize or a combat objective by one or more factions (as in Bosnia). Any move on the part of the intervention force affects the local balance of power and the prospects of one or more factions. In such a difficult environment, the intervention force is partial to the civilian, noncombatant population of the country and to administering relief, using the minimum amount of force authorized and necessary to achieve its objectives. It may take limited offensive measures to counter a particular party that is threatening the mission.

In practice, however, limiting humanitarian intervention to safeguarding civilian food and medical supplies has proved difficult. Increasingly, particularly in civil conflicts, one faction or another often comes to believe that the interdiction of humanitarian supply lines can serve its military and political objectives. When this happens, the humanitarian forces seeking to protect the civilians eventually become a party to the conflict. The international community faced this problem in Somalia, particularly when the leadership of UNOSOM II identified the local faction controlled by General Aideed as an element that was disrupting the humanitarian mission. Thereafter, General Aideed was directly targeted for attack, and the operation crossed the line that separates peace operations from combat operations, entering the realm of low-intensity conflict. The operation explicitly relinquished its neutrality and became a combat operation, although this was not recognized by the leadership of the operation at the time, and UNOSOM II was not reconfigured or rethought as a combat operation. (A more detailed discussion of UNOSOM II is contained in chapter 3.)

In Bosnia, the humanitarian operation has been a continuing pawn of war, along with the civilian population. Actions, and inaction, have been interpreted in partisan fashion by all of the local parties to the conflict. The vulnerability of UNPROFOR units to escalating retaliatory measures from local ground forces kept the United Nations and NATO from using the air power at their disposal either to enforce the mandates that they have been given or to act in self-defense.

Humanitarian interventions are complicated by multiple relief groups whose presence may predate military intervention and whose protection may have been the proximate cause of that intervention. These organizations, even those nominally part of the U.N. system, march to their own drummers. They may need the military for security but cooperate only reluctantly, and they may have pre-existing security arrangements with local "protectors" who may be reluctant to give up this source of income.

Relief organizations include U.N. agencies such as the High Commissioner for Refugees (UNHCR), the Children's Fund (UNICEF), and the World Food Program; national relief and development agencies; regional organizations' relief agencies; private relief groups (CARE, Save the Children, and hundreds of others); and local grass-roots political organizations. The simple presence of all these organizations adds complexity and further distinguishes humanitarian intervention from a traditional combat environment. The peace force must interact with them to coordinate activities, share information, and often to conduct combined operations (e.g., to escort relief convoys). The actual aid-givers may require direct assistance with transportation and communications, in addition to intelligence briefings and medical support. All these interactions are conducted outside standard military procedures developed for combat operations.

Peace Enforcement

Peace enforcement operations use coercive force to suppress conflict in an area, creating a *de facto* cease-fire to protect noncombatant populations and facilitate the opening of negotiations among local factions. Peace enforcement can be distinguished conceptually from traditional combat by its objective of general conflict suppression, as contrasted to battlefield victory against a defined enemy. By comparison to traditional combat, its rules of engagement will seek to minimize casualties, both its own and those of the indigenous population (whether combatant or civilian). In consequence, it may place much greater reliance on non-lethal weaponry and strict, thus limiting rules of engagement. An enforcement operation may also attempt to maintain an appearance of impartiality, using necessary force against any faction violating an imposed cease-fire.

Other types of operations can evolve into peace enforcement if the intervenors possess the resources and political will to escalate their involvement and decide to suppress or stop conflict through the use of coercive force. Peace enforcement need not derive from humanitarian operations, however. It may be the international community's response to the general collapse of governance in a country or to genocide. For instance, during the recent episode of civil war in Rwanda (1994), one option considered by the U.N. Security Council was to use a peace enforcement operation to stop the fighting and ethnic massacres. If the warring parties were forced in this manner to step back from the single-mindedness of active warfare, a reasonable, negotiated settlement may have been possible.

Implementing a peace enforcement mandate generally requires military superiority over combined local forces. In practice, while such superiority may suppress organized, conventional combat, it requires accompanying diplomatic action to resolve underlying disputes, lest fighting re-emerge at lower levels in the form of guerrilla or terrorist activities. Ultimately, the successful conclusion of such an operation must entail some form of political settlement. Simply suppressing warfare is not sustainable in the long run and should not be viewed as an end point. The underlying political or social conflict must be resolved.

Another type of peace enforcement operation is just beginning to take conceptual form in the present multilateral intervention in Haiti. The purpose of this intervention was to restore democracy and, by doing so, stop the human rights violations of the *de facto* regime. This type of operation can be categorized as peace enforcement (conflict suppression) if one views the intervention as designed to suppress and eventually eliminate an illegitimate regime's domination of a society, without forcing a regime change through traditional warfare. The Haiti operation differed from traditional combat in that the United States did not plan to destroy the local armed forces unless challenged by them as the legitimate government was restored.[3]

The Tasks of Peace Operations

Most of the tasks assigned to the military component of peace operations are part and parcel of normal military functions. However, as the Army's peace operations field manual states, "units selected for these duties require time to train and prepare for a significant number of tasks that may be different from their wartime METL [mission essential task list]."[4] Some of the tasks will be new to the military unit while others will simply require modifications of traditional military tasks.

New Tasks

As table 1 illustrates, some tasks of peace operations—relating mostly to interactions with local civilians, the parties of the dispute, and other elements of the peace operation—are not common in traditional combat operations. Combat operations seldom require intricate interaction with civilians—at most, the military may help evacuate civilians from the battlefield. In peace operations, however, the military may be required, *inter alia*, to control crowds and administer the distribution of humanitarian relief. In a hostile environment or other situations where nonmilitary providers are scarce, the military may be tasked to prioritize humanitarian relief needs, transport and protect the relief supplies, and distribute them in an orderly manner.

Negotiating with local peoples on the tactical level—including local armed elements— is always part of this job, either as an explicit objective, or as an implicit requirement to increase the safety of one's forces. (In contrast, combat forces do not negotiate with opposing armed elements but attempt to destroy them.) These negotiations are likely to be conducted by company commanders, battalion commanders, or senior battalion staff officers. At the troop level a different type of negotiation is required. As soldiers are conducting other duties, it is likely that they will be called upon or find themselves in situations in which they must arbitrate local disputes or fights concerning a range of issues from the trivial to vital. This task resembles the role played by police responding to domestic disturbances—determining the real situation and then defusing the tensions through discussion or argument.

TABLE 1: *New tasks*

Negotiate tactical Status of Forces Agreements (SOFA)with local leaders
Mediate or act as an intermediary in disputes between factions
Arbitrate local disputes or fights
Administer local justice codes
Prevent refugee flows
Conduct resettlement
Administer humanitarian relief operations

It should be noted that although the tasks requiring interaction with civilians are not included in the METL for most units, the new tasks are not totally foreign to military personnel. Military officers and NCOs receive professional training on management and leadership techniques and during their normal garrison duties acquire much practical experience in the "people skills" required for peace operations. Some formal training might assist in bridging these common-sense people skills to negotiating tasks for peace operations.

Tasks Needing Some Modification

Many tasks of peace operations are similar to combat tasks, but to the different environment and objectives of peace missions require appropriate modification, as shown in table 2. These tasks relate primarily to the use of force and the requirement for restraint in peace operations. For instance, and ironically, precision marksmanship is more important in a peace operation than in combat. Forces engaged in peace operations are more likely to engage a hostile party in the midst of noncombatants much more often than a combat soldier does. This reality reduces the menu of weapon systems available for peace operations, as most are not highly discriminate. For example, in traditional combat, incoming artillery or mortar fire is commonly countered with an immediate return barrage of artillery fire that covers a broad area. The typical and usually appropriate response in a peace operation is to evacuate the area under fire if possible, take cover if unable to evacuate, and initiate communications with the offending party to negotiate a cease-fire. If all these measures fail, the peacekeepers may resort to a limited retaliatory attack—utilizing only the most discriminate of weapons—with the intention of de-escalating the engagement.

Recent experience in Somalia has demonstrated other combat tasks that need modification for peace operations. Peacekeepers conducting a cordon-and-search, a common combat task, must be less aggressive and less destructive than if they were operating in combat. In a peace operation, for example, a door should not be blown open, the accepted technique in combat. Rather, occupants should be persuaded to open the door even though this is time consuming. Collecting and analyzing military intelligence information—another task in common with combat operations—are essential for humanitarian intervention and peace enforcement. For these operations, however, human intelligence frequently will be more valuable than that from other sources, and appropriate modifications should be made to the collection plan.

TABLE 2: *Tasks requiring modification*

Marksmanship
Coordinate military activities with U.N. agencies, private organizations and local factions
Establish static defenses
Collect intelligence
Disarm local factions
Cordon and search
Seize buildings

As already discussed, the multinational aspect of peace operations and the numerous nonmilitary organizations active in the theater greatly complicate command and control and other aspects of the environment of peace operations compared to combat operations. The tasks related to the presence of multiple agencies in the theater are primarily liaison, coordination, and conduct of combined operations with other non-military organizations. Present methods of coordination simply need to be modified and expanded to be more appropriate to the peace operations environment.

The Mix of Tasks Required for Peace Operations
Most importantly, force planners should consider the unique mix of tasks required for peace operations and the respective weights within the mix. Present force structure and force utilization

techniques derive from the assortment of tasks inherent in combat, and as table 3 indicates, the assortment prevalent in peace operations is different than those of combat.

Because peace operations are largely reactive operations, military forces are engaged in proportionately more passive or defensive tasks than in combat. For example, psychological operations and informational activities are vital because of the environment of peace operations. Also, forces in peace operations spend a lot of time guarding facilities and escorting convoys.

TABLE 3: *Prevalent tasks*

Guarding facilities
Self-protection in static positions
Escorting and guarding convoys
Negotiation, mediation, arbitration, diffusion of tension
Civic action
Providing humanitarian assistance
Psychological and informational operations
Police duties
Providing logistics support to nonmilitary organizations
Civil affairs interaction in local political processes
Area and route reconnaissance

Logistics networks are often more complex in multidimensional peace operations and humanitarian intervention than in combat. Combat logistics typically is a two-way street, with most traffic moving from the rear to the front with "back-haul" to the rear. Usually, convoys require minimal security until they are close to the front since friendly forces control the rear area. Finally, in combat, transported supplies are for the military only. Conversely, in contemporary peace operations the logistics flow may be much less linear. From ports of entry, supplies may fan out to many population centers.

In humanitarian interventions, convoys must always be protected. Supplies are provided to disparate military forces, civilian operational components, other civilian organizations, and the local civilian population. Other tasks more prominent in peace operations include antiterrorism and antitheft measures, liaison with the local population and authorities, land mine removal, media relations, and civic works, such as rebuilding roads or establishing schools. Police functions may also devolve upon peacekeepers who deploy into a post-conflict situation—functions made more complex and politically sensitive by the lack of recourse to traditional "army of occupation" procedures or legal code.

Conclusion

Thus, while not totally unique, the peace operations environment and the tasks required of forces operating in that environment are somewhat different from those encountered in traditional combat environments. This is not to suggest that specialized forces are required to successfully conduct such operations; the record attests to the fact that well-trained and disciplined, general-purpose combat forces can accomplish all peace operations requirements. However, the chances for success with minimal risk of casualties and collateral damage can be improved with prior planning, training, and, where necessary, specialized equipment.

Notes

1.   See chapter 3 for a discussion of the importance of adjusting to changing circumstances in peace operations.

2. A description of the authors' definitions for peace operations was first published in Pamela L. Reed, William J. Durch, and J. Matthew Vaccaro, *Handbook on United Nations Peace Operations*, (Washington, DC: The Henry L. Stimson Center, April 1995)

3. Once the threat of coercive force was effective in obtaining a negotiated settlement, the Haiti operation shifted from peace enforcement to multidimensional peacekeeping since the forces were present in a consensual environment to ensure the implementation of a peace accord.

4. Department of the Army, *FM 100-23 Peace Operations*, December, 1994, 86.

3. LESSONS OF THE PAST:
Experiences in Peace Operations

Christine M. Cervenak

In developing recommendations for improving the performance of the U.S. Armed Forces in peace operations, the Commission on the Roles and Missions of the Armed Forces (CORM) devised a systematic approach to learning from the past. Under this approach, several peace operations case studies compiled by the RAND Corporation were analyzed following the steps contained in the "Protocol for Peace Operations Case Studies" (see appendix). The protocol served as a framework for analyzing peace operations and was designed to draw out lessons that are specifically relevant to U.S. military activities in the area.

The peace operations case studies used in this process were not limited to those in which the United States participated directly. Instead, a wider net was cast in order to capture lessons from peace operations conducted by others as well and to comply with the Commission's legislative mandate to examine the experience of other nations.[1]

Following a general review to determine the most significant issues, the analytical approach to the case studies ultimately focused on four central questions:

Christine M. Cervenak is an international lawyer with extensive experience with U.N. operations in Central America and the Middle East. From 1987 to 1990 Ms. Cervenak was an attorney-advisor in the Office of the Legal Advisor, U.S. Department of State. She is a former Visiting Fellow at the Human Rights Program at Harvard Law School.

- What factors seem to account for the success or failure of a given peace operation?
- In what ways and to what extent, if any, did participation by U.S. forces affect the outcome of the peace operation?
- What consequences did U.S. participation have on U.S. defense capabilities?
- Faced with the choice of participating in peace operations, what do the case studies tell us about tradeoffs and other issues that U.S. policy makers must confront?

Case Studies and Analytical Methods

The cases chosen for analysis meet the definition of peace operations set out in Army Field Manual FM 100-23, *Peace Operations*; Joint Pub. 3-07.3, *Joint Tactics, Techniques, and Procedures for Peacekeeping Operations*; and, *The Clinton Administration's Policy on Reforming Multilateral Peace Operations*. They fall within "The entire spectrum of activities from traditional peacekeeping to peace enforcement aimed at defusing and resolving international conflicts." [2] As noted in the previous chapter, there are substantial differences in the requirements and tasks for different types of peace operations. The principle cases include peace operations in: the Congo (ONUC, 1960-63), Cyprus (UNFICYP, 1964-present), Cambodia (UNTAC, 1992-93), Somalia (UNITAF, 1992-93 and UNOSOM II, 1992-95), Croatia (UNPROFOR, 1992-present), and Bosnia-Herzegovina (UNPROFOR, 1992-present). A few other cases were examined and discussed to confirm the conclusions drawn from these cases or to illustrate specific points; however, these will not be discussed here except in passing.

All the cases involve military organizations with the capability to use force, at least to a limited extent, although this and other capabilities may not be equal to mission requirements. The operations examined in these studies occur in an actual or potential threat environment, although at least some of the parties to the conflicts gave nominal consent to the operations. The forces participating in the operations are multinational and are nominally impartial, although not all participants share the same goals and objectives as a basis for participation[3].

Accounting for Success and Failure

As noted in the introduction to this chapter, the first analytical question concerns those factors that contribute to success or failure in peace operations. In viewing the case studies through the lens of the Protocol, specific observations emerged. To be sure, defining the criteria for determining whether a peace operation is a success is complex and goes beyond the traditional measures of military success, such as destroying enemy formations or seizing ground. Among the more significant factors that influence success and failure are:

- The degree to which operating force capabilities fit the missions prescribed by the mandate
- The extent to which operating forces are attuned to operational dynamics and the ability of the force to respond to significant changes in an effective and expeditious manner
- The ability of the force to obtain and/or maintain the consent of the warring parties and local population.

These factors are interrelated. An operation that lacks appropriate capabilities, for example, may be unable to respond effectively to changes in the operational environment, or it may lose the consent of a population that fears it may not be adequately protected. Similarly, exogenous pressure to change various aspects of the mandate could cost the consent of one or all of the parties to the conflict and leave the peace operations force inadequately equipped to deal with new requirements. Relevant examples from specific peace operations, presented in turn, will serve to bring each of the factors into sharper focus.

Fit

The fit between capabilities and mission requirements is crucial to success. Not surprisingly, analysis indicates that success depends on a match between mission requirements and the capabilities of the forces involved. At the outset,

41

decisionmakers must be clear about what they hope to accomplish with military forces in a peace operations. In other words, they must select political objectives that can be readily translated into military missions and goals. While peace operations can facilitate agreements among the parties to the conflict (as shown by the operations in the discussion below as well as in the cases of Namibia, Mozambique, and El Salvador, for example), it is important to keep in mind during this process that, there are also limits to what military force in peace operations is capable of achieving, depending upon the type of operation undertaken.[4] For example, although military force can seldom resolve the predicaments that led to the crisis in the first place, it can help to prevent further deterioration. In short, the military may be able to stabilize crises and separate warring parties, but as a rule, the military cannot solve underlying political, social, or economic problems. To expect that is to expect too much of peace operation forces.

In creating conditions in which those problems may be solved by other elements, however, it is important to ensure that forces are capable, ready, and robust. How much the military can accomplish with respect to its mandate is determined by the capabilities it brings to the operation. Usually, the choice of capabilities is not for the military to make. Although the military may influence the decision, ultimately they come to the operation in the numbers and with the equipment specified by the civil authorities that send them. These specifications may (or may not) be appropriate to the environment, the risks, and missions at hand.

Decisionmakers must thus take into account the capabilities of the force they are willing to commit and either limit the policy objectives set forth in the mandate and missions[5] of the force accordingly, or provide additional resources to bring missions and capabilities into a synchronous arrangement. Some examples that illustrate the effects of matches and mismatches are worth considering.

Cyprus.[6] The United Nations undertook operations in Cyprus in the hopes of reconciling or ameliorating the differences between the island's Greek and Turkish residents. The two- phase U.N. operation in Cyprus illustrates how capabilities influence achievement of mandate objectives. In United Nations Peacekeeping Force in Cyprus I (UNFICYP), 1964 to the Turkish intervention in 1974), military forces were governed by a rather vaguely worded mandate for the force to "use its best efforts to prevent a recurrence of fighting and, as necessary, to contribute to the maintenance and restoration of law and order and a return to normal conditions."[7] U.N. Secretary-General U Thant framed the specific tasks for UNFICYP under this mandate, based on his assumption that Cyprus should and could be united under one government, even if that goal required some amount of coercion.

However, UNFICYP's capabilities and resources were not equal to the task implied by this assumption. In the end, the UN forces on Cyprus lacked sufficient military power to compel warring parties to agree to submit to a government imposed upon them. It simply was unable to accomplish tasks that required applying military pressure to ensure cooperation between the feuding parties for success (e.g., facilitating the return of Turkish Cypriots to government and reviving meetings between Greek and Turkish Cypriots). Despite its failure in the larger sense, UNFICYP had a limited amount of success in realizing goals that were within its resources. For example, it was able to establish a UN liaison to Greek and Turkish Cypriot police and could conduct at least limited inquiries into serious incidents.

In UNFICYP II (from the 1974 Turkish intervention to the present), the operational mission was more limited than called for by the UNFICYP I mandate and force packages were more easily structured to accomplish the tasks contained in those missions. Essentially, the mandate was to position U.N. forces between the parties along the "Green Line," a division that occurred as the two ethnic groups separated in the wake of the Turkish invasion—the Turkish Cypriots fleeing toward the invading forces and the Greek Cypriots away from them. The UNFICYP II mission takes into account the existing separation, and peacekeeping forces are not charged with trying to change this arrangement, nor are they structured to do so. Instead, commensurate with their mandate, they have the capabilities necessary to oversee the status quo and have been relatively successful in doing so.

Somalia. Operations in Somalia included the First United Nations Operation in Somalia (UNOSOM I), which our analysis did not examine.[8] Instead, the focus was on the U.S.-led United Task Force (UNITAF), an operation conducted for humanitarian purposes, and on the Second United Nations Operation in Somalia (UNOSOM II), which had much broader aims. The Somalia experiences illustrate the difference between operations in which capabilities are matched to missions and operations that are underresourced. In fact, in UNITAF capabilities were greater than required to fulfill the mission. In contrast, there was a negative, ultimately disastrous mismatch for UNOSOM II. UNITAF, an operation conducted in a nonpermissive environment to open the ports and roads to permit delivery of humanitarian aid, had great, perhaps overwhelming, combat capabilities more than adequate to accomplish these objectives. The sheer size and professional quality of the force may have made accomplishing UNITAF tasks much easier. Also, U.S. political and military leaders resisted attempts to expand operational objectives to include clan disarmament, an activity that might well have overtaxed the capabilities of the force and certainly increased the risk.

In contrast to UNITAF and with significantly less U.S. involvement and more limited military capabilities, UNOSOM II, had more ambitious objectives— assist the factions to implement the Addis Ababa agreements (e.g., all heavy weapons to be placed under the control of an international monitor), which implied reconciliation of the factions within a new central government, and capture faction leader General Mohammed Farah Aideed. These objectives were expansive to say the least. While military forces could establish some of the preconditions for their achievement, it was up to the Somalis themselves—perhaps aided by skilled diplomats rather than soldiers—to reconcile with each other. Given the capabilities of the U.N. forces and the contributing governments low tolerance for risk, reconciliation was extremely difficult, if not impossible, without the consent of all warring factions. Unfortunately, this was not always clear to decisionmakers, who seem to have assumed that available forces were daunting enough to achieve the objectives.

In retrospect, it is apparent that the UNOSOM II objectives were far too ambitious for the available forces. The substantial military capabilities required to disarm unwilling clansmen and capture a popular leader simply were not available, and the military resources that were available were often not well synchronized with diplomatic efforts. The dynamics of the situation should have indicated to decisionmakers that either more robust forces were required, or the mandate requirements had to be reduced to match them to onhand capabilities.

Croatia. Like most of Yugoslavia, Croatia was populated by more than one ethnic group, primarily Croats and Serbs. Tensions between these groups escalated in the weeks before Croatia declared independence in June of 1991. Before this declaration, Serbs in Krajina took steps toward declaring their own independence from Croatia. The Yugoslav Army intervened on behalf of the Croatian Serbs in early July. Fighting continued at various levels of intensity until November of 1991 when, under considerable diplomatic pressure, all parties to the fighting agreed to an unconditional cease fire and the presence of UN peacekeeping forces. The cease-fire, like so many in the Balkans, immediately broke down, to be resurrected in December. In February of 1992, the U.N. Security Council (UNSC) established the United Nations Protection Force.

Under its initial mandate, UNPROFOR I operations in Croatia were to "create conditions of peace and security required for the negotiation of an overall settlement of the Yugoslav crisis."[9] At the outset, UNPROFOR I, lightly armed and described as an interim force, was to accomplish several objectives:[10] oversee demilitarization or disarmament of Serb forces in the UN

Protected Areas where it was deployed (the UNPAs, basically Serb-occupied parts of Croatia, from which UNPROFOR takes its name); protect persons in the UNPAs from armed attack. If fighting were to break out or tensions were to come to a head between ethnic groups in the UNPAs, the force was to interpose itself between the opposing forces; assist humanitarian agencies; and later, in 1994, maintain a presence in the buffer area formed when Croats and Krjina Serbs agreed to separate their forces.

UNPROFOR I was successful initially in establishing weapons collection points and received some heavy weapons from the Krajina Serbs, largely because the Serbs were willing to surrender them. In the end, however, lightly armed UNPROFOR I failed to protect the populations in the UNPAs, to protect non-Serbs from forcible expulsion from Serb-controlled areas, and to protect Serbs from invasion by Croatia.[11] Without substantially more robust military capabilities and the will to use them, the United Nations was helpless to prevent the disruptive actions carried out by all parties, such as Serbian evasion of demilitarization by creating "special police" and other units equipped as light infantry, programs of "ethnic cleansing," and Croatia's invasion of Sector South in January 1993. Its helplessness was easily discernible, especially to those it was mandated to protect, a fact which may have had a bearing on levels of consent as we shall see.

Although UNPROFOR's rules of engagement authorized it to prevent incursions into the UNPAs, it was too weak militarily and too thinly deployed to apply force successfully.[12] Its task to protect civilian populations required "a larger and more capable combined armed force for external security and an extensive civilian police component for internal security." [13] Additionally, UNPROFOR was not able to prevent forcible expulsion and politically motivated crime in the UNPAs, since UNPROFOR had no authority to investigate such incidents. UNPROFOR could only monitor investigations by Serb police, who were either disinterested or pressured by Serb authorities not to investigate.

Bosnia-Herzegovina. UNPROFOR's operation in Bosnia-Herzegovina is yet another illustration of the importance of a "fit" between mandate and force capabilities, as well as the limitations of military force. UNPROFOR operations in Bosnia grew gradually out of operations in Croatia. Through several resolutions, the Security Council gave UNPROFOR a fourfold mandate in Bosnia: to implement the agreement of the parties to open Sarajevo Airport; to facilitate and deliver humanitarian aid; to enforce a no-fly zone; and to protect safe havens or areas.

Although there have been some isolated and limited successes, UNPROFOR has not been robust enough to succeed in fully carrying out its various tasks. For example, it has not been successful in securing the routine transit of humanitarian aid convoys through Serb-held territory. Serbian forces have impeded convoys, including those supplying UNPROFOR, at will and for months at a time. Also, UNPROFOR has not succeeded, with limited exceptions, in protecting the populations of safe areas.[14]

Security Council resolutions passed in response to the situation in Bosnia have invoked Chapter VII of the U.N. Charter, "implying [the Council's] willingness to at least consider peace enforcement."[15] However, peace enforcement usually requires substantial combat forces and UNPROFOR is not large enough, nor is it appropriately armed, to conduct peace enforcement successfully, particularly in light of the size and armaments of other parties to the conflict that make it difficult for UN peace operations forces to protect even themselves. The lack of capability undermines any suggestion that UNPROFOR might undertake peace enforcement missions. And, there has been no political agreement among members of the Security Council to make such a decision and to provide the necessary forces.

Each of these cases describes the results of mismatches between capabilities and missions. When such situations occur, some sort of transition must occur. Transitions must also occur when unexpected changes occur during peace operations.

Adaptability

Because peace operations are dynamic, success often hinges on understanding operational feedback and rapid and effective response to changes in the nature of the operation, regardless of the source of those changes. Unanticipated requirements are characteristic of peace operations. Conditions at the beginning of the operation will change, as they do in almost every type of military operation. Changes requiring an operational transition may occur because of:

- Changes in the facts on the ground, usually for the worse, over which the operating force may have no real control
- Failure to achieve initial objectives, which were important precursors to follow-on objectives
- Exogenous events that change internal conditions.

Whatever the source of the change, operating forces must "see it coming" and respond appropriately.

A successful process has three parts, all of which are interrelated. Success turns on establishing reliable feedback mechanisms, understanding the significance of the information they provide, and judiciously responding to new conditions in a timely manner. Feedback mechanisms include local sources of information which may be direct in nature (e.g., discussions with local interlocutors) or indirect (e.g., changes in the behavior of the local populace toward the peace operations forces). Feedback may be provided also by implicit or explicit changes—or apparent changes—to the mandate prescribed by the UNSC. Officials on the ground should be aware of potential changes and think through the consequences in advance. Usually, information will be available from a number of sources and may be conflicting. Military commanders and civil officials must be attuned to these sources, share information, apply judgment as to what the information really means and what the ramifications are likely to be for the operation, and take appropriate actions.

How peace operations forces react to changes once they are aware of them is critically important. There are essentially four options for decisionmakers to choose from:

- Fight: change to peace enforcement (but this avenue usually marks the failure of the peace operation)
- Withdraw: acknowledge the failure of the operation (but political authorities are usually reluctant to do so)
- Temporize: buy time in order to adapt (but there is a danger of becoming more deeply and expensively committed to increasingly risky operations)
- Adapt: change objectives and/or capabilities (but this may require negotiating a new mandate).

All these choices have been selected at one time or another and sometimes the choice involves more than one option. Since peace operations are preventive operations, choosing the wrong option may lead to escalation of the initial conflict into a major regional conflict, requiring greater risks and investments, or to a humiliating defeat with far-reaching effects. As in any military operation, anticipating change is important, as is thinking through the range of possible responses early on and their likely effect, given the capabilities available to the force. It is worthwhile to explore some of the transitions that have occurred in the past and their effects.

The Congo. The 4-year United Nations Operation in the Congo (ONUC), which began in 1960, was one of the earliest UN peace operations and enjoyed mixed success. In brief, ONUC came about in response to fighting between Belgian and Congolese troops who had mutinied against their white officers immediately following independence of the Congo from Belgian colonial administration. ONUC's formal mandate from the UNSC, expressed in several Security Council resolutions, was fleshed out by wideranging political and military objectives, defined by U.N. Secretary-General Dag Hammarskjold. These objectives included ensuring the departure of Belgian troops, expelling foreign mercenaries from the Katanga Province and ensuring the independence and territorial integrity of the Congo, all of which it was able to do. However, it was not successful in preventing civil war, obtaining a stable democratic government, and restoring discipline and effectiveness to the Congo's military, tasks that were part of the mandate.

The Congo was typical of most military operations: the situation in the area of operations changed almost as soon as the operation began. The civil war that ONUC was charged with preventing began within 6 weeks of the ONUC's arrival and changed the environment in which the original mandate was to be carried out.[16] In addition to changes in conditions within the area of operations, there were changes as well as in the position of the UN Security Council, which adopted Security Council Resolution 161 in February 1961. This resolution exacerbated the situation on the ground because it urged reorganization of the Congolese Army, something the Congolese central government viewed as U.N. interference in its internal affairs. As a result, a crisis occurred that might have been averted had more attention been paid to available feedback, and that crisis threatened the willingness of the central government to continue to consent to ONUC operations. Because some degree of consent is of utmost importance in all peace operations, the unanticipated action-reaction dynamic set into play in the Congo threatened the entire operation. Clearly, the situation required operational transitions by forces engaged in peace operations.

However, apparently no one gave much thought to the range of possibilities and how the United Nations might respond to them. When civil war occurred, it became clear that the peacekeepers were ineffective against determined resistance unless reinforced. In light of this, and because the United Nations could not garner the international support needed to carry out broader aspects of the mandate, transition choices were limited to changing the objectives of the operation or withdrawing. Success was redefined in much narrower terms, which called for little more than the expulsion of foreign mercenaries from the Katanga Province and the preservation of the territorial integrity of the country. While not the preferred option, the change of objectives allowed for some good to come out of the operations as a whole, without overextending ONUC forces or demanding from them results beyond their capability to provide.

Cambodia. The United Nations Transitional Authority in Cambodia (UNTAC) was deployed to assist in implementing the Paris Accords, agreements subscribed to by the warring parties to end the civil war in Cambodia. The original mandate included requirements to conduct free and fair elections, oversee the installation of the newly elected government, assist in establishing the conditions necessary for relief efforts, and disarm the warring factions consistent with the accords.

In Cambodia, as in the Congo, a radical change in conditions on the ground precipitated by elements of the population prevented UNTAC from carrying out disarmament of the warring factions, considered a key ingredient of success to end the civil war as called for in the 1991 Paris Agreement. Many believed that without it, ending the civil war and electing an effective government were impossible. Armed bands, it was reasoned, could prevent the election altogether or, if dissatisfied with the results, plunge the country back into civil war. (In fact, in light of the failure of disarmament efforts, the success of the elections and the elected government over the long run still remains to be seen.)

The Party of Democratic Kampuchea (PDK)[17] derailed disarmament when it denied UNTAC access to areas within its control and refused to take part in the cantonment process designed to lead to disarmament. The implications of this course of action were discerned by U.N. leadership in Cambodia. After the demobilization and disarmament process broke down, UNTAC changed its objectives, rather than allowing the operation to come apart in a futile attempt to force disarmament with the relatively small number of forces available. A decision was made instead to fulfill the second requirement: creation of a national government of reconciliation through free and fair elections.

Given the absence of peaceful conditions in the country and a willingness to disarm, UNTAC's military switched its focus to supporting the work of other components, particularly to providing security to the electoral component and assisting the police component. As a result, holding the election became a viable goal despite the failure to disarm all warring factions. Peacekeepers provided security for the election itself, as well as protection to electoral workers during the entire electoral process (e.g., for voter education and registration work). This election was of considerable value and relieved some of the strain on the military forces.

However, the failure of the disarmament process also made the work of UNTAC's police component much more difficult and dangerous than planned and led to another change in military missions. Criminal activity was carried out by bandits who, when disarmament was abandoned, remained more heavily armed than the UNTAC personnel. The military therefore supported the police component to supplement its firepower and deter criminal activities by making them more dangerous for the perpetrators. Military forces conducted (or assisted the police in conducting) antibanditry patrols, assisted with security duty at political rallies and during the civic education programs of the electoral component, and assisted police at checkpoints to confiscate illegal weapons.

UNTAC's willingness to modify its missions and goals in order to pursue equally important objectives did much to ensure that those objectives—particularly holding elections on schedule—were accomplished, at least in part. Instead of attempting to force disarmament, UNTAC reorganized its forces and assigned new tasks without changing the basic character of its activities by engaging in coercive acts to force recalcitrant factions to lay down their arms. In the end, UNTAC accomplished the major goal of free and fair elections of a Cambodian government, something that most likely would not have occurred had UNTAC not recognized the changes in the situation and decided against pursuing a goal no longer attainable. Whether this government survives in a country where opposition elements remain heavily armed remains to be seen.

Croatia. Unlike the Congo and Cambodia, where local situations changed independently of direct actions by intervening forces, in Croatia, UNPROFOR's activities—or rather its lack of capability to act as it was mandated to do—changed the situation on the ground. This change resulted in a *de facto* modification of the operation's goals. UNPROFOR, as noted above, was tasked to demilitarize and protect Serbs residing in portions of Croatia from attack by Croatians. Clearly it was not strong enough to guarantee Serb security and it contributed to the insecurity of the Croatian Serbs in Krajina by partially disarming them. This made the Serbs appear vulnerable, and the Croats took advantage of what they saw as an opportunity to gain the upper hand. When Croatia attacked Croatian Serbs in January 1993, the Serbs recovered their arms from UN collection points and blamed UNPROFOR for their initial setbacks. After this episode, UNPROFOR could no longer pursue its demilitarization objective, which was no longer possible to achieve with the available U.N. forces.

Cyprus. UNFICYP faced major shifts in objectives with the 1974 Turkish intervention that resulted in the *de facto* partition of the island. In this case, as in others, the primary choices were to force a return to the preintervention conditions in order to correspond to the original objectives or to change those objectives to fit the new reality. Like UNTAC, the UNFICYP also chose to modify its goals. Fundamentally, the mission changed from policing the island to the less arduous one of simple interposition along the buffer zone between Greek and Turkish segments of the population. Because this zone reflected the refugee flows, there was no need to use massive force to establish or maintain it. Because fewer troops were needed to carry out what amounted to an observation mission, UNFICYP force strength could be decreased significantly.

Somalia. In Somalia, the UNOSOM II peace operation ultimately responded to the need for transition by withdrawal. With the further deterioration of the situation in 1994, particularly when the factions refused to respect their commitment to disarm voluntarily and with Aideed's offensive in Mogadishu, it became clear that UNOSOM II was unable to carry out its mission without substantial reinforcement. By October 1994 it was clear that the operation was moribund, and the Secretary-General recommended termination of the operation by March 31, 1995.

These examples indicate that achieving success across a broad spectrum in peace operations is problematic at best. However, in order to realize some return on initial investments and to contain potentially dangerous situations (both on the ground and to prevent external opportunistic powers from meddling), decisionmakers must expect drastic changes from the outset. When they occur, the best course of action seems to be to modify goals and objectives to preserve chances of attaining some goals and retaining the consent of at least some of the parties to the conflict.

Consent

Transitions may be required as a result of changes in the level of consent of the actors in the conflict. Consent is more of a dynamic process than a condition or end state, and it will change over time. The initial level of consent may be influenced by internal changes, by outside events, and by the actions of peace operations forces and local responses to them. Or consent may have been inaccurately assessed at the outset. The importance of consent to predicting and responding to transition suggests that the maintenance and management of consent should be a key objective for operating forces. This is illustrated by the experience of peace operations forces in several cases.

The Congo. In the Congo, the forces learned early that the consent of the central government to ONUC's operations was insufficient, because in the midst of civil war that government did not speak for all interested parties, particularly those in Katanga. In effect, the experience in the Congo illustrates the fact that consent occurs at several different levels. ONUC, for example, needed to garner the consent of many local parties—some of which were at odds with the central government—while maintaining the consent of the central government, and the consent of the central government was not easy to maintain. In fact, the government initiated a harassment campaign against ONUC after the passage of the February 1961 resolution calling for a reorganization of the Congolese military.

The breakup of the central government into factions complicated consent building and maintenance greatly. Not only was maintenance of consent on the ground more complex, but UN member states had different opinions as to which faction should be recognized as representing the government, and thus cultivated to gain its consent. The relationship between the eventual central government and the United Nations deteriorated to the point where the ONUC garrison at Congo's main port was attacked by forces operating under government control. Later, relations between ONUC and the government improved, in part because of internal political developments, and in part because of the shared objective of expelling foreign mercenaries in Katanga.

It is worth noting that while consent at the national or strategic level was often thin or nonexistent, that was not always the case at the local or tactical level. In some cases, the negotiating skills of participating U.N. forces were effective enough to attain the consent of local factions to their presence and operational goals, an important feature. For example, the Nigerian contingent was successful in restoring some stability to North Katanga, mainly because of its skillful and repeated negotiations with local leaders.

Somalia. In Somalia, transitions among the stages of the mission there, from UNOSOM I to UNITAF, to UNOSOM II (with U.S. participation) to UNOSOM II (without U.S. participation) were marked by changes in the level of consent of the factions on the ground. When U.S.-led UNITAF arrived (with overwhelming force compared to that of the rival clans), clan leaders, including Mohammed Farah Aideed, felt compelled to give at least grudging consent in the face of a credible, if implicit, threat of coercion. "Uniquely in the history of peace operations, UNITAF maintained consent by making the parties believe that opposition would be futile."[18] Aideed and others withdrew this consent after most of the UNITAF forces left the country. In fact, 1 month after UNOSOM II took over, Aideed's followers assaulted U.N. forces at various locations. However, it is difficult to discern whether the erosion of consent occurred because of a decrease in military power in U.N. forces, or whether consent waned because of lackadaisical efforts to maintain it and the attempt to isolate Aideed from the political process designed to establish a new government.

Croatia. In Croatia, withdrawal of formal consent to the mandate helps to explain specific failures in the peace operation. Maintaining consent was crucial to accomplishing UNPROFOR's mandate to oversee demilitarization in the UNPA's and protect persons there from armed attack. Until January of 1993, Croatian consent was manifest in the fact that, despite local violations, Croats generally respected the cease-fire, but in January 1993, Croatia violated it, entering the Sector South and adjacent "pink zone." This prompted the Croatian Serbs to break the cease-fire under the justification of self-defense in the absence of credible U.N. efforts to protect them. They recovered their heavy weapons from dual-lock storage that had been monitored by UNPROFOR, established an army, refused to cooperate with U.N. police monitors, and continued to forcibly expel non-Serbs. When consent of both parties was withdrawn—as evidenced by violations of the provisions of the cease fire—failure was inevitable.

The precise reasoning that led to withdrawal of consent cannot be known at this point. However, UNPROFOR's activities under its mandate, as well as its lack of combat ability and authority to coerce the parties, very likely contributed to the breakdown. The Croatians had become impatient with UNPROFOR's inability to protect non-Serbs in the UNPAs and lack of progress in restoring Croatian control of critical areas. The Croatian Serbs believed the U.N.-monitored demobilization made them vulnerable to attack, and UNPROFOR was clearly unable to defend them once attacked.

Consent was restored somewhat in March 1994, with the externally brokered cease fire agreed to by the Croatian Government and Croatian Serbs. However, the effects of the initial loss of consent are more or less indelible. UNPROFOR's credibility in the future has been called into question. Restored consent may be only a "consent of convenience," to be withdrawn as the opportunities to do so are presented to one opponent or the other.

Bosnia-Herzegovina. The U.N. response to changes in consent in Bosnia-Herzegovina was managed poorly. None of the parties seems to have fully supported UNPROFOR's mandate at the outset. All the parties violated their agreements to one extent or another, with Bosnian Muslims being the most supportive and the Bosnian Serbs the least. The Serbs, for instance, frequently challenged UNPROFOR to see how far it could be pushed. When UNPROFOR did not respond to these provocations with force, except under the most dire circumstances, it may have left the Serbs with a feeling of contempt, rather than consent, for U.N. presence.

Although it remains unclear whether the parties to the conflict ever truly consented to UNPROFOR's operations in the first place, there is room to question whether UNPROFOR adequately cultivated their consent. Given the evident problems with consent, the Security Council may have exacerbated the issues by focusing on the wrong remedial actions. Instead of looking for ways to gain acceptance from the warring parties for the existing goals and objectives, the UNSC gave more responsibilities to UNPROFOR. Many of these would do little to improve consensual relations. For example, the Council authorized the use of coercive measures, despite the problems and limits inherent in the use of such measures given UNPROFOR's capabilities and the situation on the ground. Moreover, consent is based on persuasion, not compellence. Coercive measures usually do not gain the willing acceptance of those against whom they are directed.

These factors or variables seem to be the most important in accounting for the success or failure of the operations highlighted in the case studies. That is not to say that they are the only variables; there are others, but they do not seem to have the same impact.

Peace Operations and the United States

Although U.S. involvement in these operations varied, it is important to look at what U.S. decisionmakers can learn from them. Such information is a key factor in determining what the United States might be called upon to provide in future operations and the sorts of tradeoffs that might be required should the United States decide to become involved. Three questions are worth examining:

- How did the United States contribute to these operations and what effect did that have on the outcome?
- What were the effects of participation on overall capabilities?
- What balance must be struck between U.S. involvement and the likelihood of operational success?

In what ways and to what extent did participation by U.S. forces affect the outcome of the peace operations?

For the most part, the United States was not directly involved in the ground operations of any of these forces, save UNITAF and UNOSOM II. However, the United States did provide other kinds of support for some of the case study operations. For example, for a variety of reasons the United States declined to participate in ONUC directly, although it did provide airlift for other forces. In dealing with the conflict in the former Yugoslavia, the United States, through NATO, has helped to enforce the no-fly zone, the safe areas, and the embargo in the Adriatic Sea. In the post-Cold War environment, the United States faces increased political pressure for leadership and/or participation in peace operations. This is particularly true where the actual use of force may be needed. But it is also true of other situations. Technically speaking, the United States contributes unique capacities to peace operations in the areas of technical intelligence, communications, and force projection capabilities (i.e., strategic lift and long-term logistics support) that cannot be provided by any other nation on the same scale. Other capabilities are either possessed by other countries or could be developed by them with modest assistance. This suggests that, from the technical perspective, direct U.S. participation in the more traditional peace keeping operations may not be necessary, or at least may be kept to a minimum. However, larger operations under more risky conditions will probably not be undertaken without substantial U.S. support. The necessity of a proper fit between the mandate and the mission capabilities and for adaptability as circumstances change helps to explain why other nations seek U.S. involvement.

In order to manage pressures on the U.S. to participate in peace operations, the United States could assist other nations and international organizations to improve their peace operations capabilities. Building and strengthening peace operations-specific military capacity in other countries and through multilateral organizations will expand U.S. options when faced with the pressure to participate in a specific peace operation.

The Somalia case study illustrates the political and technical significance of U.S. participation in peace operations, particularly as they become more complex and demanding. "During UNOSOM II, the United States provided the Special Representative of the Secretary-General and contributed combat units under national control that were essential for peace enforcement. . . . Had the United States not assumed [a leading role in UNITAF], the Security Council would very likely have confined its efforts to security of humanitarian aid and observation of the parties' ephemeral cease-fires."[19] Despite the presence of forces from ongoing UNOSOM I operations when U.S. forces arrived in Somalia, without U.S. participation in UNITAF, the distribution of food and other aid would have been at the mercy of faction leaders intent on using food to undermine enemies and promote their own power. In short, little would likely have been accomplished, and additional thousands may have perished.

What consequences does U.S. participation have on U.S. defense capabilities?

In the earlier operations, the answer is that it had little effect at all because participation was on a small scale. Looking at U.S. involvement in recent peace operations, particularly Somalia and Haiti, the overarching lesson that emerges is the necessity to prepare for peace operations as part of the normal military planning and training process. It may be true that where objectives were not accomplished, failure was not due directly to a lack of trained personnel. But that does not mean that better trained and prepared forces would not have done more to achieve success.

Based on the foregoing, what tradeoffs and other issues do U.S. policy makers face with respect to participation by U.S. forces in future peace operations?

The answer to this question lies, first, in the relationship between U.S. participation and the probability that the peace operation will be successful. At the outset, it is important to understand that while U.S. participation in peace operations may be required, it does not guarantee success, particularly in light of the complex political factors that imbue any peace operation scenario. At the same time, the United States is likely to be pressured to participate in peace operations specifically where there is a higher risk of failure. But, from a military standpoint, peace operations are not always managed well. Military leaders required to participate in coalition operations prefer to participate with competent partners, yet troop contributors are too often determined by political concerns, not by the real capabilities of their troops or the needs of the mission. In Cambodia, for example, the Bulgarian forces have been described as composed of police and paroled prisoners who were inadequate as soldiers.

The Bangladeshi and Pakistani forces apparently showed little initiative and avoided patrolling in areas under their responsibility. Yet all of these contingents were politically acceptable to the factions involved and available.

Another management problem is inadequate coordination within the peace operation. In fact, while participating in UNOSOM II, the United States conducted operations unilaterally with little coordination with the U.N. forces. This failure to coordinate has been blamed by some for the lack of prompt relief of U.S. forces during the October 3, 1993, incident when 18 U.S. soldiers and probably several hundred Somalis died.[20] Of course, operational security must be preserved, and plans should not be shared with all contingents under every circumstance, especially given the fact that some forces are of questionable competence. Where that is the case, then the tradeoff facing U.S. decisionmakers involves making the peace operations force more robust, possibly at the expense of reduced capability for other missions, in order to guarantee the safety of the force.

A second important question derived from the RAND analysis is, what effect do peace operations have on the ability to execute two, near simultaneous major regional conflicts (MRCs)as called for by the present force-sizing criteria? Drawing on the case studies, the response prompts a number of important observations. First, civilian decisionmakers and the U.S. Armed Forces are presented with various general options vis-a-vis peace operations in light of the two MRC requirement:

- Not to become involved in peace operations
- To become involved and live with the current "stretch" of forces and strategy
- Become involved but degrade U.S. capability to execute a two MRC strategy.

Each of these options entails some unpleasant results, and each has strategic ramifications far beyond the operation at hand. For example, participation may head off a much larger conflict, or, conversely, failure to participate may mean that the U.S. forfeits its leadership role.

Second, as long as peace operations are a secondary or tertiary mission, unplanned-for tradeoffs will arise each time the United States involves itself. Military leaders are currently hard pressed to make sound compromises in order to dispatch forces for peace operations. Choices must be made on the spur of the moment and there is a chance that both civilian and military decisionmakers may try to do peace operations on the cheap—which is likely to lead to forces incapable of achieving operational goals or responding adequately to situational changes.

Third, proper training for peace operations entails developing a truly robust force. Forces must be combat ready, flexible, and able to adjust to changes in the peace operations environment, particularly if success is likely to be determined by the force's ability to adjust to such changes. As the cases show, the mission that was planned for may not be the mission ultimately executed. Training for robustness requires a broad range of training: crowd control, negotiation, liaison, relations with NGO's, minimal use of force and restricted firepower. In Cambodia, for example, the ability of the military component to provide support once the disarmament process fell apart showed some of this "robustness." Peacekeepers were assigned to assist other components, providing security and support to a wide range of activities, from working at UNTAC's refugee reception centers to supporting civic education campaigns.[21]

But producing robust forces with the capabilities needed for the sorts of large, risky peace operations in which the United States is likely to be called upon to participate may mean curtailing training for other operations, as Vaccaro and Raach discuss in their chapters. Resources are finite. Training, the stock-in-trade of the peacetime military, uses resources at a fast pace. Time for training is also finite. When forces are training to improve their capabilities for peace operations, unless there is an overlap in skills (discussed in other chapters), they cannot train adequately for more conventional operations.

Degradation of readiness remains a contentious issue in the United States and appears to be far more complex and subtle than it appeared to be before the current post-Cold War experience. The duration of involvement of American troops and the type of peace operations actually engaged in certainly affect ongoing training requirements for other military missions once they return. However, the effects of this may be relatively short lived.

Conclusion

There are important lessons to be learned from the studies of prior peace operations, both at a policy level and from the perspective of detailed military operations. This chapter has attempted to extract a few of the more salient themes from a handful of cases studied by RAND. They were useful in informing the work of the CORM as it proceeded to its recommendations. However, there is a larger universe of cases and issues to be tapped, and the learning they offer changes over time. The unfolding tragedies in the former Yugoslavia will require much more time and distance before clear lessons can emerge. It appears from current analysis that certain missions are internally contradictory and cannot succeed, but that story is far from ended. Moreover, a great deal more experience in post-Cold War peace operations and case analysis will be required before generalizations can be made with confidence.

Nevertheless, it is important to document experiences and contemporaneous impressions of peace operations in detail, and to test hypotheses that seem to make sense. The Department of Defense consistently tries to incorporate the lessons from past experience into future policies and operations. The post-Cold War peace operations experience is new and extraordinarily varied thus far. Given the growth in internal conflicts throughout the world, and the uncertainty and range of potential options, such case analysis, though imperfect and incomplete, is crucial to the process of formulating effective policy and operational responses.

Notes

1. Public Law 103-160, as amended by Public Law 103-337.

2. U.S. Government, The Clinton Administration's Policy on Reforming Multilateral Peace Operations (Washington, DC: The White House, May 1994).

3. Peace operations case studies in this chapter are drawn directly from RAND's data base of case studies, updated for the CORM on an expedited, informal basis. Because time limits imposed on the CORM in the establishing legislation did not permit a completely new analysis of each operation, RAND drew on existing case studies, analyzed them in accordance with the protocol, and identified and assessed key variables. At the CORM's request, RAND conducted a workshop in Santa Monica, CA, at which the protocol, the cases, and the apparent lessons that could be drawn from them were discussed by a panel of expert analysts over a 2-day period in January 1995. RAND presented a briefing recounting the results and recommendations of this workshop in February 1995. The briefing was presented to a wider audience at a round table seminar at the Institute of Peace in May 1995. Events occurring after this time affecting ongoing peace operations are not included here, although we have seen nothing in the intervening period that would cause us to change our conclusions.

4. See the discussion in chapter 1 of the types of peace operations and the relationship of the military to other elements of power in resolving underlying problems.

5. As used in this chapter, the term "mandate" refers to the directions provided to the military force by the United Nations Security Council or other authorizing body. "Missions" are military requirements that must be accomplished in order to fulfill the mandate.

6. A full description of the cases cannot be included in the space available. However, many excellent references are available which provide great detail on these cases, including many excellent publications by RAND, the Institute of Peace, and the United Nations.

7. U.N. Security Council Resolution 186 of 4 March 1964. Ambiguous mandates appear to be the norm in peace operations. Ambiguity can result in confusion and exacerbate a capabilities-mission mismatch, or it can provide considerable operational latitude for forces on the ground.

8. UNOSOM I was conducted beginning in the late spring of 1992 and had the mission of securing humanitarian aid. The success of the

operation was pinned to the consent of the warring clan leaders, which proved elusive. Before the operation accomplished much, UNITAF arrived and assumed the mission.

9. U.N. Security Council Resolution 743 of 21 February 1992.

10. In addition to a lack of combat power , UNPROFOR also lacked reconnaissance elements, transportation, and the logistics support required for effective operations.

11. UNPROFOR I was successful in overseeing the departure of the Yugoslav Army from Krajina and in establishing collection points for heavy weapons.

12. Pursuant to Security Council resolution 743 of 21 February 1992 and the peacekeeping plan outlined in a 1991 report of the Secretary-General, UNPROFOR I would use force only in self-defense while carrying out the mandate.

13. RAND Project Memorandum, May 1995.

14. "The notable exception was Sarajevo where a NATO ultimatum, implemented on the ground by UNPROFOR, almost completely abated Serb bombardment of the city. But in two other 'safe areas,' Gorazde and Bihac, UNPROFOR and NATO failed to stop Serb offensives." RAND draft case study of Bosnia-Herzegovina, 3.

15. RAND Project Memorandum, May 1995.

16. U.N. Security Council res. 161 of 21 Feb. 1961.

17. "PDK" is the new name adopted by the part of the Khmer Rouge remaining loyal to Pol Pot.

18. RAND Project Memorandum, May 1995.

19. Ibid.

20. Some after action reviews have faulted the lack of coordination between the U.S. and the forces of other nations for not having readily available reaction forces that could come to the aid of forces engaged with members of Aideed's clan.

21. It should be noted, however, that one of the criticisms of UNTAC was that peacekeepers did not have the necessary training specific to the Cambodian situation, and the training level varied considerably among national contingents. "As a result, training deficiencies may have contributed to the poor impression often made by UNTAC troops on the Cambodian population." RAND Memorandum, Cambodia, 14.

4. PEACE OPERATIONS AND COMBAT READINESS

J. Matthew Vaccaro

Defining Readiness

The global demand for U.S. participation at some level in peace operations is likely to persist. Such participation can promote and protect U.S. interests, but peace operations address less direct and immediate threats to U.S. security than those addressed by plans for major regional conflicts. As such, they necessarily receive a lower priority than combat operations, but some arrangements must be made if the demands of these new types of missions are not to detract from U.S. readiness for more traditional combat missions. U.S. forces are most likely to participate in humanitarian interventions or multidimensional peacekeeping missions that require specialized capabilities that only the United States can provide, or a demonstration of U.S. leadership and commitment that draws together and sustains a multinational force. If the record of the past 5 years is any indication, some fraction of U.S. combat forces will be involved in these missions for the foreseeable future.

The purpose of measuring readiness is to gauge the ability of the Armed Forces to accomplish the tasks they are given. During the Cold War, the tasks of the U.S. Armed Forces consisted

---

J. Matthew Vaccaro is a Senior Analyst at DFI International, a research and consulting firm in Washington, DC, where he manages studies on conflict resolution.

primarily of deterrence and combat. However, it is becoming increasingly evident that in the post-Cold War environment, the armed forces will be required to conduct a variety of operations that are challenging, yet short of war. In fact, operations other than war have become more and more frequent over the last 5 years. There has been considerable discussion that a result of this increase has been continued strain on funding that has reduced combat readiness. The degradation of combat readiness caused by the shortage of funding could be avoided by adjusting accounting techniques to insulate training and maintenance funds from contingency funding, raising the level of funding built into the Operations and Maintenance account (OMA) for contingency operations, or ensuring quick and complete supplemental authorizations.

Because readiness has become an important public issue, it is worth reviewing what the term implies. The Joint Chiefs of Staff define readiness as the ability of forces, units, weapon systems, or equipment to deploy without unacceptable delays to perform the tasks for which they were designed. Under the present definition, four areas are specifically evaluated when determining readiness: personnel availability, equipment availability, equipment serviceability, and training proficiency. The last factor is the most subjective and is determined by the commander's assessment of the unit's proficiency to accomplish its assigned tasks. When a unit is assigned a mission, that mission is broken into discrete tasks that are compiled into the unit's mission essential tasks list (METL). The commander's subjective evaluation of readiness is based on his or her judgment about the unit's ability to accomplish each task listed in the METL.

Higher readiness is always desirable. Unfortunately, high levels of readiness are difficult to maintain because adequate resources are not always available and military skills atrophy without regular practice. Because the services cannot train for all contingencies all the time, the key issue is to identify the tasks for which they must be prepared, the level of readiness desired with regard to each task, and a method to shepherd resources appropriately to achieve that level of preparedness.

Each unit within the Armed Forces is given a readiness rating. A "C-1" rating, the designated target for all units, indicates that the unit has the required personnel and equipment resources and is judged able to undertake all of its assigned wartime missions. C-2 indicates that a unit has its assigned resources and is able to accomplish most of its wartime missions. C-3 indicates a unit has most of its resources and is judged able to accomplish many, but not all, of its wartime missions. C-4 indicates that the unit does not have its required resources and cannot undertake its wartime missions[1].

The evaluation system is limited. It does not measure the ability of units to accomplish all tasks of peace operations, just as it is not geared to evaluate joint warfighting skills. If resources and skills needed for combat were entirely interchangeable, this would not pose a problem. However, since peace operations do entail tasks that are sometimes significantly different than combat operations, the current deficiencies of the system may pose a risk to personnel deployed to a peace operation and could impede the United States ability to accomplish its objectives in such operations by presenting a false picture of unit proficiency (see chapter 2).

The Effects of Under-funding Contingency Operations

DOD contingency operations are funded from the OMA, which have little, if any, funds built into them to pay for unforeseen operations. When the actual costs of contingencies exceed the budgeted amount, DOD must request a supplemental authorization from Congress, a process that can take months. In the interim, funds shifted from OMA must be used to pay for the contingency. If the Congress chooses not to authorize supplemental funding, or authorizes only partial funding, then DOD must reduce OMA spending further to accommodate for the shortfall. Even when supplemental funds are approved, the delay built into the process may cause a cash-flow problem. When this occurs, as it did in the fourth quarter of FY 1994, combat readiness is degraded. Training activities were canceled and repair parts were not purchased because funding had been redirected to contingency operations. Any unforeseen contingency, and not just peace operations, can drain resources and thus degrade readiness if not replaced quickly.

The Effects on Readiness of Preparing for Both Peace Operations and Combat Operations

Preparing for peace operations rather than training solely for combat operations will cause some erosion in combat readiness. The amount of erosion is unknown and probably cannot be measured accurately. However, to a large extent, the amount of degradation depends upon the degree of difference between a unit's combat tasks and those practiced for peace operations. For example, some units' training for both types of operations would be quite similar, since the tasks they conduct in both cases are similar. Transportation or civil affairs units could add nuances to existing combat training and become qualified for peace operations with little degradation in their combat skills. Some combat units, on the other hand, conduct a far smaller proportion of their combat tasks in peace operations. Soldiers are seldom required to use their weapons, apply massive force, coordinate artillery fires or large-scale maneuvers, or do tank-on-tank engagements during most peace operations. Because training time and resources are finite, adding peace operations training for these units will detract from training on combat tasks, thus reducing combat readiness.

However, dividing training time and resources among the different types of missions should not be considered a zero sum game. All the fundamental military skills learned from combat training will facilitate development of peace operations competency. Further, some combat skills will be enhanced through training for and doing peace operations (chapter 5).

The Effects of Serving in a Peace Operation on Combat Readiness
During peace operations, as in any type of operation, individuals become ill, get injured, or otherwise are removed from service; some military equipment is lost or expended; and other equipment becomes unserviceable. Thus, operations of any type, including rigorous training, can degrade combat readiness in the first three areas: personnel availability, equipment availability, and equipment serviceability.

The effects of serving in peace operations on the fourth factor of readiness, proficiency in combat tasks, are not well documented. Anecdotal evidence suggests that during peace operations certain individual and unit combat tasks are seldom exercised and become atrophied. These skills are not necessarily lost; they simply need to be practiced more often than allowed during a peace operation for the individual or unit to retain proficiency. Commanders of light infantry battalions returning from Somalia, for example, reported that their units most needed to practice company-level fire and maneuver techniques and battalion-level coordinated attacks. Company commanders placed greatest emphasis on weapons requalification and firing of all weapon systems, especially crew-served weapons— mortars and antitank weapons— that had not been used during the peace operation. Battalion staffs needed to re-hone fire coordination skills and synchronization of combat elements on the battlefield—skills that are some of the more difficult to maintain whether or not a unit deploys to a peace operation. Generally, commanders believed that, their units would regain proficiency in these combat skills, following a period of refresher training.

On the other hand, the evidence suggests that proficiency in some combat skills is actually improved by peace operations service, and tasks common to both peace operations and combat are the most likely to show improvement. For instance, mobilization and deployment for a peace operation also enhances a unit's ability to mobilize for a combat operation. Other combat skills or tasks practiced, and presumably improved, during peace operations include living in an austere or dangerous environment, force-protection techniques, construction of fighting positions, observation and reporting, small unit operations, intelligence collection and analysis, communications, and almost all logistic operations. Peace operations may also improve individual and unit abilities to adapt to unusual situations and may increase unit discipline—certainly beneficial to any military operation. This is discussed in more detail in chapter 5.

Another aspect of combat readiness implicit in the present readiness measurement system but difficult to measure is the degree of "warrior spirit" embodied within a unit. Presumably, more of this is better should the forces be employed in combat. Some have argued that the mind-set of peace operations— typified as one of restraint—degrades the "warrior spirit" and should such restraint be inculcated into the Armed Forces, it would reduce their ability to win on the battlefield. An opposite opinion holds that exposure to the complexities of peace operations develops more mature leaders and the capability to respond more nimbly to any situation, be it combat or something else. Because this issue bears directly on the question of whether deployed forces can be expected to transition from peacekeeping to enforcement and perhaps back again, it requires greater empirical study, drawing on other countries' experiences and training simulations.

In order to document the effects of peace operations on combat readiness, the data used to compute unit readiness both before and following deployment to a peace operation should be evaluated. By comparing a commander's before-and-after assessments of task proficiency and studying the commander's plan to rectify any deficiencies, the Armed Forces could better understand the effects of peace operations service on combat readiness. Any conclusions should be categorized by type of unit and type of mission, but it should be noted that the present readiness measures, focused on combat, do not provide all the information one would desire. Conclusions from them may therefore not yet be fully reliable.

Alternative Means of Participating in Peace Operations

Several means are available to facilitate effective U.S. participation in peace operations without diminishing the preparedness of U.S. Armed Forces for combat operations. As the Army downsizes to 10 active divisions, and Marine Corps end strength stabilizes at 174,000, any significant participation of U.S. troops in peace operations will degrade the ability of the Defense Department to meet the force requirements of two, nearly simultaneous, major regional conflicts (MRCs) as called for in the National Military Strategy. This impact might be reduced by activating equivalent units from the reserve component to meet standing MRC requirements. However, large-scale or frequent activations of the reserve component would be unrealistic politically, in the absence of an immediate security threat to the United States. Consequently, it behooves the Department of Defense to examine alternative means of fulfilling the requirements posed by peace operations, three of which are:

- Creating a pool of U.S. active forces that prepare for peace operations as a secondary mission
- Restricting U.S. contributions to providing specialized capabilities, equipment, and training
- Depending more on designated reserve component forces and civilian contractors.

Create a Pool of Forces Designated for Peace Operations

DOD would designate a pool of active units and assign them the mission of conducting peace operations in addition to their traditional missions. The units would add peace operations tasks to their METL and train on them in the normal training cycle. The readiness indicators for the units would be broadened to include measures of preparedness for peace operations. Within the pool, a rotation system would be developed to designate which units would be tasked first for any peace operation. The rotation system could function similar to the "Ready Brigade" system used within the 18th Airborne Corps to designate the order that combat elements would be called into a contingency mission. However, the rotation should not shift as often as the "Ready Brigade" rotation does. A longer period would allow units to become more proficient in peace operations tasks. For instance, if a light infantry division held the designation as the "first" unit to be called for any peace operation for an entire year, it would be able to hone its peace operations skills while focusing less on combat tasks. Other units in the pool could continue to emphasize combat training until just before receiving a higher designation for peace operations. Forces outside of the pool would not be required to participate in peace operations under normal circumstances and would thus be able to focus training solely on their traditional combat missions.

The peace operations pool might be a mix of combat, combat support, and combat service support forces. Ideally, the pool should provide a menu of force packages to conduct most peace operations. Most of the forces in the pool would be drawn from the active component to ensure an ability to respond quickly to contingencies. Types of units in short supply in the active component, such as psychological operations and civil affairs units, could be augmented with reserve units. If repeated activation of Reserve units seems unlikely, the Army should consider increasing the quantity of these units in the active component to cover both combat and noncombat contingencies adequately.

Usually, peace operations are multilateral endeavors but, on occasion, the United States may choose to conduct such operations on its own. The "pool" alternative ensures preparation for both types of scenarios while allowing the vast majority of the U.S. Armed Forces to focus solely on traditional combat tasks.

The burden of peace operations on U.S. forces could be reduced further by developing a complete package of equipment specially tailored for use in peace operations. The kit could be prepositioned in a particular region or kept ready at an air base for transport to a mission area. Upon receiving orders for a peace operation, a unit would leave most of its combat equipment at its home base and marry up in-theater with the peace operations kit. The kit would provide capabilities not included in most units' combat equipment. An example would be armored HMMWVs[2], which offer greater mobility and protection to light infantry battalions and greater urban mobility to units normally equipped with heavier, less agile combat vehicles.

For training purposes, additional kits could be maintained at training centers. This approach would reduce wear and tear on a unit's regular combat equipment and thus reduce one effect of peace operations on combat readiness. Units conducting peace operations also would have ready access to specialized equipment appropriate to their particular mission. Most of the specialized equipment could likely be procured or leased from commercial venders and would probably be cheaper than combat stocks.

Restrict U.S. Contributions to Multinational Peace Operations to Critical Capabilities, Equipment, and Training

The United States would limit its participation in multinational peace operations to providing only critical capabilities, equipment, and training that otherwise might not be available; the U.S. would not provide combat forces. It would instead be prepared to provide strategic lift, intratheater lift, close air support, intelligence products and/or units, theater-level communications, civil affairs units, or psychological operations units. Some of these contributions would involve U.S. troops on the ground and concomitant risks to their safety in some instances.

To eliminate even that risk, the United States could provide equipment and training to other troop contributing countries or to the international organization conducting the operation—e.g., provide military or off-the-shelf civilian communications equipment and any necessary training, in lieu of deploying a U.S. signals battalion. Armored vehicles, water purification equipment, and field medical supplies could also be maintained and supplied in accordance with prior agreements; some division of labor to this end might be established among the industrialized countries. A similar arrangement might apply to training of other countries' forces for peace operations, over time increasing the number of countries capable of conducting particularly difficult operations and lessening the demand on U.S. forces.

Two drawbacks of this alternative should be noted: it would not maintain a trained capacity within the Armed Forces to conduct unilateral peace operations effectively, and the absence of U.S. units from multinational peace operations, as envisioned in the second variant of this alternative, could well discourage other states from participating in them as well.

Make Greater Use of Reserves and Contractors in Peace Operations

The United States could reduce the burden of peace operations on active forces by replacing active forces with a mix of active and reserve units and contractors as soon as conditions permit, allowing at least some active forces to return their focus to combat operations. In some cases, it would be feasible to use reserve forces from the start of an operation, for example, where the starting date of an operation is known some months in advance. In other cases, reserve units and contractors could be phased in once the active forces had established a somewhat secure environment.

Figure 1 indicates how the force mix could change according to the urgency and duration of the mission, and the level of danger to deployed forces. Currently, any mission with a short "lead time" would require use of active forces, some of which could be deployed within hours. The lead time necessary to engage contractors would be longer, but could be reduced if the United States were willing to keep some contractors on retainer for peace operations. Certain capabilities would then be available on demand and on short notice, as has been the case for the Civilian Reserve Air Fleet and for sealift. Reserve forces tend to require the longest time to mobilize, but that might be reduced if the U.S. were to make regular use of the Nordic reserve volunteer

FIGURE 1. *Force mixes*

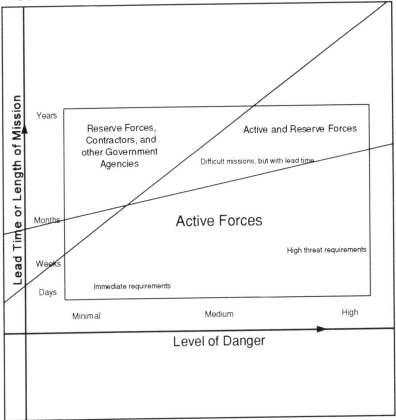

model now being implemented for the U.S. contribution in the Multinational Force and Observers (MFO). The level of danger inherent in an operation would, of course, influence this mix. In dangerous operations, commanders would likely feel more confident with active forces alone, at least on the ground and for the first few months of the operation and perhaps for the entire mission. If reserve components are to be used for the more dangerous operations, stepped-up training will be needed, as demonstrated during *Desert Storm*. Contractors are unlikely to commit to the most dangerous types of missions, and if they do, hazard-related costs are likely to escalate sharply.

Figure 2 illustrates the approach of using mixed active, reserve and contractor units, with two actual operations as examples. The MFO, a non-U.N. traditional peacekeeping operation in the Sinai Peninsula, grew out of the 1979 peace agreement between Israel and Egypt and had the luxury of substantial lead time in its deployment. Although peacekeepers in the MFO have faced minimal danger from the start, for nearly 13 years the U.S. military contribution to the mission has been met by rotating one battalion at a time into the region from high-priority infantry units, including the 101st Air Assault, the 82nd Airborne, and more recently, the 10th Mountain Division. In January 1995, a newly formed, all-volunteer infantry battalion composed mostly of reserve personnel (based roughly on the Nordic peacekeeping model) rotated into the MFO mission. This transition to lower priority forces could have occurred quite some time ago. The operation's observer component, for example, has been civilian from its inception, so there is no requirement for first line forces all of the time.

The second example is the 1994 U.S. intervention in Haiti, which had a long lead time because the United States attempted to resolve the country's political crisis through diplomatic means and economic embargoes for more than a year. Initially, the mission was considered dangerous because the reaction of Haitian armed forces and paramilitary organizations could not be predicted. Forced entry was avoided, however, and over time the mission became less dangerous, and doable, in principle, with contractors and reservists. Under a phased-transition concept, the Defense Department could have begun preparing reserve forces for eventual deployment into Haiti as soon as active forces began to prepare for a possible intervention.

Reserve component forces could be made available for peace operations in a variety of ways. The President could activate preexisting units under his authority as Commander in Chief, or volunteer units could be formed ad hoc and given appropriate training, as was done for the January 1995 MFO rotation. Alternatively, the training guidelines for designated reserve units could be selectively and drastically modified to allow for a fixed-length, operational training deployment to a real peace mission.

FIGURE 2. *Risk and force mixes*

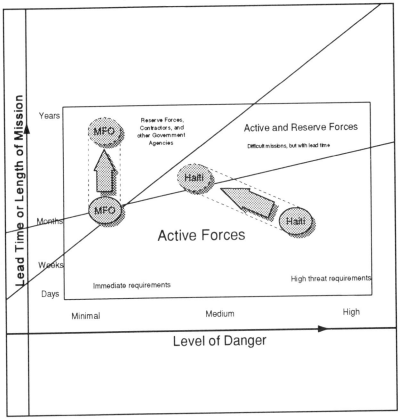

For instance, a reserve engineer battalion could be activated, given 1 month of predeployment training, and then deployed to a peace operation for 6 months. Using reserve units in this way could increase their basic operational proficiency, although long term mobilizations could effect Reserve Component recruiting and retention.

There are precedents for using contractors in peace operations. DOD contracted with several companies to provide logistical support to U.S. units in Somalia, and in the former Yugoslavia, the U.N. Protection Force has used contractors extensively as body guards and for other types of security, and for mobility, strategic lift, food service, and distribution of humanitarian relief. In general, in many peace operations the environment is benign enough that virtually all logistics functions (including provision of food, water, laundry, petroleum products, vehicle maintenance, and the like) could be procured from the private sector. Setup and operation of informational radio stations and operation of a mission's internal communications network could also be outsourced.

Operations in Somalia and Yugoslavia have demonstrated that contractors can be used even in dangerous environments. In such operations, armed forces can provide greater security for contractors doing field work (for example, delivering relief). At some point, however, in dangerous operations the expected cost of providing such protection (and the cost of hazard insurance and pay) would likely exceed the benefits of using contractors.

This alternative could greatly reduce the burden of peace operations on U.S. active forces while making more effective use of reservists. The effect on the reserves might cut two ways, however. Some reservists will be attracted to overseas deployments, while others may be dissuaded from joining a force that is likely to deploy. This effect might be mitigated by making participation in peace operations a voluntary matter, but the overall effect on recruitment cannot be estimated without further study.

Conclusion

In today's environment it is imperative that units be ready at the proper time to conduct the proper mission. In that environment some traditional combat focus can even detract from a unit's readiness to perform its post-Cold War tasks. For example, for the forces serving in Haiti, any predeployment training on antitank techniques would have been unimportant for the peace operation they are now conducting and would have taken time better spent on honing crowd control techniques.

The prevalent assumption that if a unit is prepared for combat it is also prepared for peace operations is irresponsible. Readiness indicators must explicitly measure the ability of the force to carry out each type of operation it may conduct, otherwise units may be deployed into operations for which they are unprepared. The current C-rating system could continue to be used to indicate the ability to conduct combat and a complementary rating scale could be developed to report the ability to conduct peace operations. Hence, a unit assigned both combat and peace missions would report two readiness indicators—a C-rating for combat and a P-rating for peace operations. Forces that are likely to be employed only in combat, such as armored divisions, could continue to use the present system alone.

DOD must adapt to prepare U.S. Armed Forces for these contingencies. The most effective way to provide U.S. participation in peace operations without unduly burdening active forces would be to adopt a mix of the three complementary approaches just described. An active forces pool combined with a relatively rapid transition to reserve forces and/or contractors and a specialized logistics kit for peace operations may be the most feasible alternative to sending active forces into peace operations ad hoc. Such an approach would require greater reliance on the reserves and on contractors than is currently the norm within the services. But it could reduce the consequences for the active component of numerous or long-duration peace operation deployments, while still allowing the United States both to participate in them in a worthwhile fashion and to be prepared to conduct peace operations unilaterally should that need arise.

Notes

1. A unit's overall "C" rating is based on the four evaluated areas: personnel availability (the number of personnel in the proper grades and career fields that are actually assigned to the unit), equipment availability (the amount of authorized equipment that is actually on hand), equipment serviceability (the amount of equipment on hand that is operational, and training proficiency. Although there are exceptions, the general rule is that a unit's overall "C" rating cannot exceed the lowest rating of its sub elements.

2. High Mobility Multi-Purpose Wheeled Vehicles, essentially a versatile, all-terrain light truck.

5. MILITARY PERSPECTIVES ON PEACE OPERATIONS

George T. Raach

Most studies of peace operations focus on techniques, procedures, and the reasons for success or failure. Relatively few studies examine how the military leadership perceives peace operations and their role in them, however, because it has been difficult to gain access to official positions. Some leaders seem uncomfortable with peace operations, which are viewed by a number of officers as not entirely compatible with the warrior culture. This chapter discusses the perceptions of the Military Services, as provided to the Commission on Roles and Missions (CORM), and provides a somewhat different perspective complementing other chapters.

A General Perspective

As part of its analysis of peace operations, the Commission studied the responses provided by the Military Services to various requests for information. It also interviewed and consulted a number of senior officers responsible for planning and conducting

George T. Raach, a retired Army officer, is a member of the CORM's professional staff. He has been the Military Assistant to the Deputy Under Secretary of Defense for Policy, the staff director for the DoD report to Congress on the Persian Gulf War, and a member of the faculties at the Army, Navy, and National War Colleges.

operations of all types. Perspectives vary to the extent that no single view characterizes the perception of all of the Military Departments, or the communities that make up the individual Services. Despite differences, however, there are some common threads.

The first is that service perspectives are dynamic and evolving as a result of in-the-field experiences, and after-the-fact attempts to make sense out of them. For example, some positions taken by representatives of the military at the outset of the CORM analysis changed in a matter of months. Over a longer period, speeches by senior officers given from 1990 to 1993 show a decided predilection against involvement in peace operations. During this period, speakers often made the point that the services exist *only* to fight and win the Nation's wars, anything that does not contribute to that goal amounts to a waste of resources. Today, the line is not quite so hard. Comments by senior leaders indicate that they recognize that reasonable missions go beyond *only* fighting and winning and that at least some peace operations can contribute meaningfully to national security. In response to a query from the Commission staff, for example, the Marine Corps wrote that *"peace operations* in their various forms, designed to enhance stability, prevent or ameliorate crises, and extend or enhance influence and assurance are [a] cardinal activity of the . . .Marine Corps" during peacetime.[1]

This shift indicates guarded acceptance of peace operations as legitimate requirements for military forces under certain circumstances. That does not mean that the military searches for, or embraces, opportunities to conduct peace operations. The military continues to relegate peace operations to a catch basin category known as Operations Other Than War (OOTW) and deals with them ad hoc. OOTW is a crowded category that includes a number of missions, the priority of which is constantly in flux but usually low and for which relatively little advanced programming, planning, or training is done until a crisis develops.

Still, there is a change in perspective, and it may mark a departure from the traditional cultural bias against anything that does not contribute directly to warfighting. For example, peace operations are formalized in the National Military Strategy (a document prepared by the Joint Staff), which discusses peace operations as part of peacetime engagement, deterrence, and conflict prevention.[2] However, it would be incorrect to think of this change as revolutionary in nature. The military still views peace operations as collateral functions that detract from readiness [3].

Yet to say that peace operations detract from the readiness of the services invites the question, "Readiness for what?" Despite the new tendency by some to consider peace operations within the realm of legitimate missions, for professional military officers the answer is readiness for conventional war fighting. Previously, when forced to discuss exactly how peace operations were detrimental to readiness, the services often responded in somewhat vague terms that such operations undermined readiness across the board and had very little, if any, positive value. In some cases, these views included a great deal of ambiguous, off-the-cuff analysis about undermining the spirit of the force and denying it the opportunity to practice the arts of warfighting[4].

This response has recently become more refined. All services routinely analyze their participation in various types of operations, but sometimes such analysis is more objective than at other times, and, because of concerns that a potential enemy might take advantage of weaknesses, it is rare for the services to provide the public with their conclusions about operational effectiveness. However, consistent with security requirements, a more precise assessment of the way peace operations influence readiness—particularly of ground forces—has emerged, and that assessment is worth examining because it influences how the military regards its role in peace operations.

The Value of Peace Operations

As noted, until recently the military often saw little value in peace operations. However, as the peace operations environment and the tasks required by that environment became more apparent and better understood, some positive attributes began to emerge from the military perspective. The accompanying table summarizes the effects of peace operations on several crucial readiness factors.

TABLE 1. 10th Mountain Division readiness after Haiti[5]

Super **Better Than JRTC/BCTP**	*Great* **JRTC/BCTP Level**	*Good* **Home Station Equivalent**	*Fair* **Home Station Equivalent**	**Readiness Concern**
Discipline Spirit Morale Cohesion Command & Control Staff Training Intelligence Logistics Maneuver *Infantry* *Company* *Aviation* *Units* *Military* *Police* Deployment	Maneuver-- *Brigade* *Battalion* Mob/CM/ Surv[6]	Fire Support	Air Defense	Aviation-- *UH-60* *Maintenance*

The information contained in the table is drawn from a briefing prepared by the U.S. Army's 10th Mountain Division, a unit that participated in both Somalia and Haiti and that has as much on-the-ground experience in peace operations as any military unit. It is worth examining some of these factors in more detail, keeping in mind that the 10th is designed first and foremost for conventional warfighting and assesses its readiness in those terms. (The factors shown in the table are not all inclusive; however, they do represent the more important elements that contribute to unit effectiveness.)

Five categories describe the division's readiness and are depicted across the top of the table to offer a method for comparing the value of experience in Haiti with what the division would have experienced had it remained at Fort Drum, NY, its home station, or had it participated in a major training exercise. The results shown in the vertical columns below each category could be used by commanders to make a determination about the level of training in the unit and about the effectiveness of the unit in general. These determinations would then be used to assign a "C" rating in training proficiency, one of several factors that determine the overall rating.

From a military perspective, major exercises such as those at the Joint Readiness Training Center (JRTC) and the Battle Command Training Program (BCTP) are prime events, and participation in either of them is a milestone or standard for measuring readiness. The JRTC is located at Fort Polk, LA. It provides a demanding, free-play exercise that, for most units, is the premiere annual or biannual training event. The cycle of preparation for and evaluation at the center brings units to peak levels of readiness. Scenarios at the JRTC vary according to the needs of the unit going through a "rotation," as deployments to major training centers are called. The JRTC, supported by a credible opposing force unit that is supplemented by civilian contractor role players, can conduct exercises that center entirely around peace operations. Scenarios can also portray a situation in which a unit begins by conducting a peace operation that then degenerates into conflict, thus integrating both types of operations.

Battle Command Training Program (BCTP), a program that exercises division, brigade and battalion staffs, is conducted by an independent organization. Like the JRTC, BCTP enhances the readiness of battle staffs and is capable of generating a wide variety of scenarios that can simulate various operational environments and integrate various staff functions into exercise play. It is not only the act of participating in these activities that is important. The training regimens undertaken to prepare units for participation are a serious and critical part of the overall process. In some cases, those regimens can span several months. Thus, where there is an assessment that the value is equal to or better than that obtained from JRTC/BCTP experiences, the assessment refers not simply to the 1- or 2-week training event but to a much longer preparation period as well.

Ratings equal to that which might be conducted at home station do not imply ineffectiveness. In most cases, this sort of ranking—the normal ranking for units that have not been through a major training exercise recently—simply means that some additional time and effort will be required to achieve the highest rating prior to deployment, although this effort does not necessarily require a full JRTC or BCTP regimen. When an area is rated as cause for concern, the implication is that effort and resources above the normal expenditures are required.

The column, "Super, Better Than JRTC/BCTP," has three discernible categories. The first deals with measures of unit effectiveness, the second with the ability of commanders and staffs to perform effectively, and the third with the ability of units to deploy and conduct effective operations. All three are critical measures of effectiveness.[7] These categories determine the difference between average and superior units. The number and nature of factors receiving such a rating indicates that the operational environment in Haiti afforded beneficial qualities that could not have been duplicated, even in the most realistic of training regimens.

Morale, cohesion, spirit and discipline are not easily quantified, yet they are extremely crucial to the effectiveness of any unit. Napoleon remarked nearly 200 years ago that the moral qualities are to the physical qualities of a force as three is to one.[8] If they are present in high order, then units are more likely to be capable of accomplishing the most demanding missions, regardless of adversity. Without those qualities, the best equipped units are likely to fold under trying circumstances.

Much of the business of leadership is devoted to instilling these qualities. When units prepare for a rotation at major training centers, and when they emerge from these exercises with high marks, the inculcation of these qualities are among the most valuable results. For a unit to exhibit high morale and spirit, true cohesion, and the sort of discipline that will carry it through requires accomplishing meaningful tasks in a demanding environment. Such conditions, difficult to create in garrison and training exercises alike, are a natural part of peace operations, where the environment is always challenging and the results can be gratifying. Equally important, as noted by several senior officers in conversations with Commissioners and the Commission staff, forces engaged in operations such as Haiti have a sense of accomplishment that equals or exceeds that which accompanies successful participation in training exercises.[9]

Similarly, it is difficult to create optimum conditions in garrison for exercising effective command and control and staff procedures, the second category. Home station conditions are substantially different from operational environments. While exercises can provide temporary conditions in which to practice these procedures, these are at best fleeting, contrived opportunities. Unless deployed for extended contingency operations, most Army and Marine Corps units spend the preponderance of their time in garrison settings, not in major training exercises. Although small units frequently deploy to local training areas for short periods, battalion, brigade (or regiment) and division commanders and staffs spend much of their time immersed in the administrative and housekeeping details necessary to run military installations. They rarely have the opportunity to command and control their forces in an operational setting.

While procedures for administrative control may be somewhat similar to those used during actual operations, the differences are substantial. Even during major exercises, many key aspects of command and staff work often will not approximate actual operational requirements. For example, intelligence play in exercises, regardless of attempts to make it more realistic, is nevertheless still "play." The consequences of getting it wrong may be embarrassing, but not fatal, and all concerned know that at the outset. The same may be said of logistical miscalculations.

Peace operations, on the other hand, provide a long-term realistic environment that places stress on commanders and staffs and offers the possibility of real sanctions if procedures are not carried out properly.[10] Veterans of such conditions are obviously much better prepared for conventional combat operations than their contemporaries who did not participate and whose exposure to the rigors and demands of operational venues is for shorter periods, under much less stressful and more controlled circumstances.

Certainly, not every task carried out in of peace operations approximates wartime tasks, but that does not mean that units engaged in routine patrolling or area denial tasks during peace operations do not have the opportunity to practice many of the skills that they would perform in combat. In the case of the 10th Mountain Division, infantry companies, and aviation and military police units in Haiti received better training in many of the mission essential tasks required for success in more conventional military operations than they would have received during training exercises in the United States.

One must keep in mind that not all combat missions belong to infantry units. Many of the tasks required of forces in combat fall to other arms and services, such as military police, and aviation transportation, and supply units. These forces often find the requirements of peace operations and those of conventional combat are quite similar. For these units, the requirements of peace operations can be more beneficial to long-term combat effectiveness than exercises and simulations, and the conditions under which they must perform their skills are closer to actual combat conditions than can be duplicated at training centers. Even infantry units do not spend all their time attacking hills during conventional combat operations, although attacks and defenses are a large portion of what they do. Requirements to demonstrate combat proficiency include patrolling, area denial, local security, and the establishment of defended strong points. Peace operations share these requirements and the tasks and principles involved in both environments seem to be very closely aligned.

As noted in the table, some key units benefitted extensively from operations in Haiti, notably infantry companies and aviation and military police units. This is not to suggest that these organizations could step from peace operations directly into conventional wartime operations without some additional training; except perhaps for the ready elements of the 82nd Airborne Division, almost no unit can. But it does suggest that peace operations certainly did not undermine their readiness for conventional warfare and did much to provide a firm foundation so that a minimal amount of time would be required for training before deployment to conventional combat.

Of course, not all areas receive the same benefit from peace operations. Because there was no requirement to employ field artillery fire support or air defense artillery in Haiti, training value for these units was units was about equal to what they would have received at Fort Drum. The only major concern was in maintenance of UH-60 Black Hawk helicopters. Problems here arose because these aircraft, which are the primary troop-carrying aircraft in the division, were used so extensively that, consistent with safety requirements, some periodic maintenance was deferred until the division returned to garrison.

The Adverse Impact of Peace Operations

Although there is increasing recognition of the many positive attributes of peace operations for forces engaged in them, there is also concern that peace operations have a deleterious impact on forces not directly participating in them. In its severest form, this impact takes the form of the shifting of funds in Operations and Maintenance Accounts (OMA) in response to unfunded increases in Operational Tempo (OPTEMPO)[11]. Reallocation of OMA funds has perhaps the greatest impact on readiness from the Service perspective and its effects are debilitating for all services[12]. This effect was a common complaint voiced by senior officers in all services when they commented on peace operations.

Succinctly, as stated in a memorandum from the Army's Forces Command , "A dollar of OMA is a dollar of readiness."[13] There are no monies earmarked in the budget to fund potential peace operations. As is true of other contingency operations, peace operations are, for the most part, funded after the fact by design. When the Executive Branch decides to initiate a peace operation, it must pay for the costs of that operation out of hide until it submits, and Congress approves, a supplemental appropriations request. This procedure restricts the latitude of the Executive Branch and ensures that Congress will become involved in the decisionmaking process at some point.

For most costs, out of hide means out of OMA. These accounts are used to fund training, equipment maintenance and some modernization projects. When OMA is used to pay the bills for deployed forces, there are tradeoffs in the range of activities in which nondeployed units can engage. Some activities must be cancelled or curtailed. For example, in FY94, while forces were deployed to Somalia, the Army curtailed or cancelled several major exercises, eliminated some critical training at garrisons in the United States, and deferred maintenance of older items of equipment; the Navy curtailed flying hours and deferred ship, aircraft, and property maintenance.[14]

Even when reimbursement is made through supplemental appropriations, some costs are not recouped. For example, the Army describes the system for reimbursement as having "failed to provide for timely reimbursements or reprogramming of funds, and when it has done so, it has never been at 100% of our costs."[15] The Army's Director of Strategy, Plans, and Policy also emphasized this point: "The recovery of those resources in the past has been time-consuming and often incomplete."[16]

The Army 's concerns are shared by other services. The Marine Corps was funded at less than half the level required to meet the operational demands of peace operations. [17] The Air Force, which has paid for some of the costs for peace operations using savings that resulted from early downsizing decisions, informed the Commission that if additional costs "are not addressed there will be future problems maintaining readiness."[18] The Navy also noted approximately $184.7 million in unfunded costs for peace operations in 1994 that led to cancellations of training and deferment of maintenance.[19]

The amount of money involved is not a particularly large share of the overall defense budget; peace operations are comparatively cheap when compared to conventional operations.[20] In FY92/93, peace operations cost approximately $1.6 billion and about $1.7 billion in FY94, or a little more than one-half of 1 percent of the total defense budget for each of these years.[21] (The bulk of the costs were for Somalia and Haiti.) If costs are this small, then why do the services perceive such a problem? The answer lies partly in the fact that service budgets for operations and maintenance have no room for adjustments and partly because the effects of cancelling training or deferring maintenance are cumulative. The lack of tolerance for unanticipated demands on OMA means there is no choice but to cut back on events when OMA funds are used to pay the bill for contingency operations. Although the services are selective about the events that are cancelled or curtailed, those that fall under the axe are often events with far-reaching consequences. For example, if maintenance is deferred or repair parts stocks are not replenished, then equipment most likely will not be used, or its use will be at less than optimum rates. That, in turn, will necessitate some diminution of training. Because service members expect to train at levels that ensure their success during operations, cut backs may engender morale problems and produce a lack of confidence. In extreme cases, units that require special certifications may not be trained to a level where that certification can be granted without waiver.

There are similar effects when training events are cancelled outright. A Forces Command report indicates that one of twelve major exercises was cancelled during FY94 as a result of funding constraints due to peace operations.[22] The unit most directly affected was probably a combat brigade, a unit that should have a readiness level of C-1. However, since brigades fight as part of divisions, there was an indirect affect on the parent division's capabilities, also.

It is not a simple matter to correct these kinds of problems even once reimbursement is authorized. Units training for a major exercise that is cancelled cannot simply pick up the training where they left off once new funding is received. Skills that are not used atrophy regardless of the type of unit or Service. In most cases, a unit that has had a training event cancelled must conduct refresher training—at some additional cost—to regain initial proficiency before proceeding from the point at which the cancellation occurred. Similarly, equipment on which maintenance is deferred may require extensive work later, even if placed in storage during the deferment period. For example, seals on hydraulic systems and automotive components may deteriorate leading to larger problems. Deferring maintenance or replenishment of repair parts, then, can have a cascading effect that leads to greater problems in the long run as equipment deteriorates.

To some extent, service perceptions of peace operations are influenced by the lack of prompt reimbursement and the effect upon the readiness of units. Another area of common service concern is Personnel Tempo, or PERSTEMPO, which provides a measure of the amount of time forces are deployed away from their home station. Each service has a slightly different standard for gauging PERSTEMPO, and the rate may vary among different elements within a Service. The object of the PERSTEMPO standard, in part, is to provide a target figure, usually expressed in days, that individuals will spend away from garrison for operational and training requirements.

Peace operations have extended PERSTEMPO rates in many cases. For example, in the Army, military police were averaging only 10.8 months between overseas deployments during FY94.[23] As a result of peace operations in FY94, the number of exceptions (or waivers) in the Navy for ships to exceed PERSTEMPO rates doubled when compared to FY93.[24] A Government Accounting Office (GAO) report noted that a Marine Corps unit spent 6 months deployed off the coast of Somalia, returned to the United States in June of 1994, and within 3 three weeks was deployed off the coast of Haiti.[25] The same report noted that two Air Force F-15E squadrons had been continuously deployed in support of peace operations since 1993.[26]

Several reasons spur concern about excessive PERSTEMPO rates. First, repeated extended deployments affect morale and retention and, as a result, long term readiness. A senior Army general speaking to a seminar at the Harvard Law School in November 1994 said that, while peace operations do not hurt the readiness of forces for conventional combat, they do have an effect on quality of life and ultimately on the retention of skilled service members.[27] This is not to suggest that forces are reluctant to endure the hardships associated with arduous duty, but as is true in any endeavor, too much can be debilitating, especially among service members who may not include peace operations in a list of reasons for enlisting in the first place.

Then, too, it is important to judge the impact of extensive deployments not only on the military personnel involved but on their families, also. The attitude of family members toward military service and the quality of life it provides cannot be ignored, especially with respect to reenlistment decisions. Although too early for a definitive statistical analysis of the effect of recent PERSTEMPO increases on retention, nearly back-to-back deployments of the type experienced by the Marine unit cited previously may well have an adverse effect.

Another concern is that units deployed for extended periods may not be able to complete all required training. The Air Force indicated particular concerns in this area. In a December 1994 memorandum to the CORM, the Air Force stated, "Squadrons are not able to accomplish certain events when deployed to a peace operation that are accepted indicators of air crew proficiency."[28] GAO analysis revealed that, as a result of extensive participation in peace operations "48 percent of EF-111 air crews and 42 percent of active component F-4G air crews received waivers for training requirements that they were not able to complete during the January-June 1994 training cycle."[29]

What accounts for the increase in PERSTEMPO? There are several answers. First, most of the forces, especially Army units, are drawn from the active component (AC). The only operation that involved involuntary mobilization of reserve components (RC) was Haiti in which a callup of about 1,900 was authorized. RC participation in all other operations was through volunteers, which works better with Air Force RC than with other services.[30] This means that the AC bear the major share of the burden for military requirements, and the effect can be somewhat drastic. In Somalia, for example, the Army used 100 percent of its AC general supply and air terminal movement control units, 75 percent of its AC petroleum supply companies, 67 percent of its cargo transfer companies, and 50 percent of its water purification detachments.[31] A high percentage of other available AC units (such as military police companies) were also used to support Somalia, refugee operations at Guantanamo, and then Haiti. Similar units are available in the RC. There appear to be no structural or legal impediments to mobilizing them for peace operations beyond making a political decision to do so, but that has been a difficult decision to make.

A second reason for heightened PERSTEMPO is that the military often performs activities that could be performed equally as well by non-DOD agencies and private contractors. Given the requirements of peace operations and the operational environment, the military will always have to perform some functions because only it can—for instance, combat activities—and it may have to engage in some activities because a nonpermissive operational environment precludes involvement of civilian organizations. However, both OPTEMPO and PERSTEMPO can be reduced if innovative ways can be found to broaden the base of available assets beyond those available specifically in the active component and in the Total Force in general. Additionally, at least two senior Army generals, speaking on condition of nonattribution, believe that it might be worthwhile to help improve the capabilities of various nations and international organizations. They perceive these to be investments that may allow the United States to do less in the future. While acknowledging that the United States will always have to provide some capabilities (e.g., strategic lift and satellite communications), many nations have light infantry and military police forces that, with very little training, can be made available for peace operations in lieu of American units.

The Issue of Missions and Objectives

A final issue influences how the military leadership perceive peace operations. This is the often expressed desire on the part of senior leaders to receive clear political objectives and guidance at the outset of operations. This point surfaced throughout our analysis in almost every interview and panel meeting conducted.[32]

Much of what is done at the highest levels of military strategy involves converting political objectives into military objectives, crafting a plan to achieve those objectives, and designing a force structure that can implement the plan within acceptable levels of risk. All this becomes much easier if the objectives (and the constraints and politically acceptable levels of risk) are made clear at the outset. The officer corps as a whole is concerned that peace operations are often done with vague mandates, derived from compromises and then presented to the military to interpret and execute. Succinctly, military leadership is wary of "just do something" directives. In fact, many conventional wars have been fought successfully with fairly blurry instructions from civilian decisionmakers. The Gulf War, for example, had four central political objectives. However, only the first two—ejecting Iraq from Kuwait and restoration of the Kuwaiti Government—were clear and easily measurable. The other two—security and stability of Saudi Arabia and the Persian Gulf and safety and protection of Americans abroad—were less precise and open to broad interpretation.

However, historical evidence aside, the military expects clear objectives that lend themselves to military procedures and measures of success. As much as any other factor that affects readiness, lack of clear objectives is a prime element in how the profession views peace operations. Reluctance to engage in these operations may be directly proportional to the imprecise nature of the objectives, and this is an important point to keep in mind. In the post-Vietnam military culture, using force in the absence of clearly stated policy objectives borders on the absurd to the professional military. Yet, given world conditions and the type of future disruptions to peace and stability, it will be difficult in many cases to precisely define objectives. This problem requires close cooperation between civilian and military decisionmakers and a degree of flexibility on the part of both.

Conclusion

A potential cultural shift may have begun as the military searches for relevance in the post-Cold War era. First and foremost, the military believes it exists to fight and win the Nation's wars. However, many senior officers have begun to see the efficacy of operations designed to prevent, contain or ameliorate conflict, and perhaps reduce requirements for larger commitments in more risky environments later.

Rather than blanket objections to peace operations, the military perspective is now more refined. Some aspects of these operations offer professional benefits and may actually improve force readiness for some units in some areas. Yet the services are concerned about other aspects and with good reason. Heightened OPTEMPO, lack of adequate funding, and increased PERSTEMPO potentially threaten both short- and long-term readiness. Operations without clearcut objectives are also troubling in a profession that perceives itself as having been victimized by the Vietnam War. Still, none of these facets presents insurmountable obstacles, nor are they offered by the military as excuses for not participating. The Armed Forces have engaged in peace operations despite the presence of these irritants and, if called upon, they will no doubt continue to do so. However, providing a remedy for these problems will improve effectiveness, not just for peace operations but across the board.

Notes

1. Headquarters United States Marine Corps Memorandum for the Roles and Missions Commission dated December 6, 1994, 1.

2. *National Military Strategy of the United States of America: A Strategy of Flexible and Selective Engagement* (Washington, DC: The Joint Staff, 1995), 9 and 12. See also the Clinton administration's *National Security Strategy of Engagement and Enlargement* published in February 1995.

3. Collateral Functions are functions which Military Departments perform with resources designed for other, primary activities. Unlike primary functions, collateral functions cannot be used as the sole justification for procurement or force sizing.

4. This assertion is based on the assumption that peace operation's forces somehow lack the mental agility to rapidly change focus to a conventional warfighting role. Given the high quality of the present force, the assertion is questionable and appears to have little basis in fact.

5. As viewed in May 1995.

6. Mobility (Mob)/Counter-mobility (CM)/Survivability (Surv) refer to the freedom of units to move about on the battlefield, to deny opponents the ability to do the same, and to survive various forms of attacks.

7. Equipment availability and serviceability are important measures of readiness, also. However, none of the Services provided

any evidence of equipment problems for units involved in peace operations. As is true of any type of contingency operation, units participating in them generally receive top priority for maintenance and repair parts. Thus, these units often have a higher equipment availability rate during actual operations than they might when in garrison.

8. David G. Chandler, *Campaigns of Napoleon* (New York: The Macmillan Company, 1966), 155. Other experts have made similar judgements. For example, see Clausewitz, *On War* and Allan R. Millet's and Williamson Murray's *Military Effectiveness* (Boston: Allen and Unwin, 1988).

9. Commanders in Haiti and Somalia whom we interviewed stated that, in both instances, their personnel were proud of what they did and what they accomplished. This sense was greater in Haiti, but applies to forces serving in Somalia as well.

10. Although not singled out in the table, many officers noted the value that peace operations have in training junior officers and noncommissioned officers to take initiative and to make decisions. There is a great deal of anecdotal evidence from both Somalia and Haiti that suggests, that because small units and patrols often operate at some distance from senior headquarters, lieutenants and sergeants must direct and supervise actions without over-the-shoulder prompting. There is, of course, risk in this arrangement, however, since this is the way the military culture expects its leaders to act on the battlefield, there is also great opportunity for leader development.

11. OPTEMPO refers to the level at which forces are programmed to operate. When contingency operations occur, they constitute an increase in OPTEMPO that requires reallocation of resources until supplemental reimbursements are authorized.

12. Letter from the Secretary of the Army, 2; Memorandum from the U.S. Army Chief of Staff for Operations and Plans, Subject: Army Comments on Peace Operations Team's Options, 19 January 1995, 1; Memorandum from the Department of the Navy, OPNAV N513C, Subject: Conduct of Peace Operations Affect on Navy Readiness, 8 December 1994, 1; Memorandum from the Special assistant to the Chief of Staff of the Air Force, Subject: Air Force Comments on Peace Operations Issue Group Options, 17 January 1995, 1; Memorandum from Headquarters, US Marine Corps, Subject: Peace Operations and Readiness, 6 December 1994, 1.

13. Memorandum from Chief of Staff, Forces Command, to CINC, U.S. Atlantic Command, Subject: Force Readiness Assessment to Congress, dtd 26 October 1994.

14. Ibid, 4-5. Memorandum from OPNAV N513C, 8 December 1994, 1-2.

15. Letter from General Gordon Sullivan, Chief of Staff, United States Army, to Senator John M. McCain, December 7, 1994, 2.

16. Memorandum from the Director of Strategy, Plans, and Policy to the CORM, Subject: Army Comments on Peace Operations Team's "Options" (sic), 19 January 1995, 1.

17. Memorandum from Headquarters United States Marine Corps to the CORM, Subject: Peace Operations and Readiness, 6 December 1994, 1.

18. Memorandum from Special Assistant to the Chief of Staff of the Air Force for Roles and Missions to the CORM, Subject: Impact of Peace Operations on Readiness in the Air Force, 9 December 1994, 1.

19. Memorandum from the Department of the Navy OPNAV N513C to the CORM, Subject: Conduct of Peace Operations Affect on Navy Readiness, 8 December 1994, 1.

20. Although a precise accounting has never been made available, the costs for *Desert Shield* and *Desert Storm* in 1990-91are estimated to have exceeded $57 billion.

21. Memorandum the Deputy Assistant Secretary of the Army for Budget for the Deputy Comptroller of the Department of Defense (Program/Budget), Subject: DOD Cost Reports for Contingency Operations, 18 November 1994, 1.

22. Memorandum from Chief of Staff, Forces Command, to CINC, U.S. Atlantic Command, Subject: Force Readiness Assessment to Congress, 26 October 1994, 4.

23. Ibid, 2.

24. Memorandum from OPNAV N513C to CORM, Subject: Conduct of Peace Operations Affect on Navy Readiness, 8 December 1994, 1.

25. U.S. Government, General Accounting Office, *Peace Operations: Heavy Use of Key Capabilities May Affect Response to Regional Conflicts* (Washington: Government Accounting Office, March 8, 1995), 6 (Hereinafter, GAO).

26. Ibid, 5-6.

27. CORM Peace Operations Issue Group Memorandum for Record # 10, 30 November 1994.

28. Memorandum from the Special Assistant to the Chief of Staff for Roles and Missions to the CORM, Subject: Impact of Peace Operations on Readiness in the Air Force, 9 December 1994, 1.

29. GAO, 5.

30. The Air Force has done a remarkable job of melding AC and RC roles consistent with the missions assigned to it. Other Services, faced with the need for units or large crews as compared with the Air Force are at a disadvantage if they have to depend strictly on volunteers. While the Air Force can make use of individual RC pilots, for example, the Army frequently needs entire units, all of whose members are not likely to volunteer.

31. GAO, p. 21.

32. See CORM Peace Operations Issue Group Memorandum for Record and Military Service files in the Commission's archives, part of the National Archives holdings.

6. MILITARY CULTURE AND INSTITUTIONAL CHANGE

A. J. Bacevich

Each of the American military services has evolved its own identity, a complex of beliefs, traditions, prejudices, and values deep-seated and setting that institution apart from the others and from society at large. These attributes are at the core of the service and can make change difficult. This chapter explores the impediments that face those who seek to change service concepts of identity and methods of operation. These issues require careful consideration as U.S. policy makers and military leaders ponder the roles and priorities of the armed forces in a variety of peace operations

Service Identities

The elements of Service identity are integral to its purpose and character, and that identity is utterly authentic. Although it can, with difficulty, be altered, it cannot be simply discarded. For those who devote their lives to professional military service, institutional identity is integral to their self-esteem and sense of purpose. It helps define who they are as individuals. It differentiates soldier from civilian. It causes, for example, a Marine to see himself as utterly and irreconcilably distinct from

---

Dr. A. J. Bacevich is executive director of the Foreign Policy Institute at the Paul H. Nitze School of Advanced International Studies in Washington, DC.

his Army counterpart, although both wear the same battle dress uniforms, carry the same weapons, and engage the same adversaries in ground combat.

More than mere personality, this identity takes on the characteristics of a full-fledged culture. As such, it has both positive and negative consequences. Military culture can provide a reservoir of institutional strength and continuity. Yet it can also become a source of rigidity, inflexibility, and resistance to change. Proponents of military reform—particularly "outsiders" who are working from a base external to the military itself—whose deliberations fail to account for military culture invite frustration and failure. In contrast, those whose approach to reform makes a friend of military culture enhance their prospects of success.

Cultural Attributes

What are the attributes of military culture? Three elements stand out as particularly important. First, is the image of the individual service member as passed on from generation to generation. However much recruiting jingles or ad campaigns may change, each of the services adheres to certain abiding themes in describing what individual service in that institution signifies. What is it, for example, that makes an airman an airman? For decades, the central image has been one of intimate engagement with advanced technology, of being on the frontier of applied science, and of contributing directly to the near-sacred process of strapping a pilot into a needlenosed jet poised to launch into aerospace. What makes a marine a marine? The contrast with the image of the airman could not be greater. Every member of the Corps—regardless of specialty—sees himself or herself as a member of a warrior elite. To have survived the rite of passage known as boot camp is proof positive of individual toughness and self-discipline. Beyond that, the hallmark of the marine (and of the ex-marine) is an extraordinary level of identity with the Corps and its traditions, a subordination of individual to collective norms that is all the more compelling because it is so contrary to the "typical" American character.

A second element of military culture is the service's definition of what it does or does not do. This includes both the style of warfare with which the service is most comfortable and the range of missions other than war that the service is willing to undertake, and since Vietnam, the services have been united on this count. When it comes to becoming engaged in any undertaking where political objectives are hazy, public support only tepid, the prospects for a rapid decision remote, and the risk of substantial casualties high, service opinion is unanimous: count us out. The Vietnam syndrome lives on in the American officer corps, regardless of service.

In other respects, the services continue to have very different views about how to fight and about what responsibilities beyond war to accept. Decades before the Air Force's existence as an independent service, for example, aviators argued that strategic bombing— the use of long-range, massed striking power directed against the enemy's vital centers—provided the key to winning wars quickly, decisively, and cheaply. Wielded effectively, strategic air power would make ground and naval campaigns unnecessary, and the forces raised to wage such campaigns redundant. The Air Force continues to make that argument. Persuaded of the primacy of strategic air, it only grudgingly expends resources on functions that it considers ancillary -- airlift, to cite one important example. The other services show comparable biases.

A third element is the service's perception of its relationship to civil society and to the other three services. The Navy, a self-contained force with organic maritime, air, and ground combat capabilities, typically strives to reduce any relationship to an absolute minimum. The Navy craves independence. The Marine Corps, a poor relation within the Navy Department and the Army's competitor for the ground combat role, views the interservice arena as inherently hostile. With some mix of paranoia and prudence, it sees itself as constantly fending off threats to its prerogatives if not its very existence. Since before its birth, as noted above, the Air Force has sought with great singlemindedness to establish that combat in its preferred realm has eclipsed all other forms of conflict. The Air Force pursues supremacy, the effect of which will be to render the other Services obsolete and irrelevant.

Within the Army, by comparison, orthodoxy dictates that war cannot be decided except by occupying or controlling territory, a task that only the soldier on the ground can preform. Victory requires the participation of air and naval forces, but their efforts are meaningful only to the extent that they support the G.I. toting a rifle. Under the guise of "jointness," the Army seeks to subordinate the other services to itself. Likewise, as the service with the least claim of glamour, the Army has tended to worry more than others about its relationship with American society as a whole. As a result, the Army has styled itself, somewhat fancifully, as the service that is closest to the American people. Whatever slender connection this notion may have to reality is manifested through the National Guard. When it comes to viewing reservists as prospective wartime partners, Regular Army attitudes generally vary between skepticism and downright hostility. On the other hand, the National Guard does provide the Army with roots in local communities, and it is tolerated on that basis. Thus, the Army has generally found reason to celebrate the Guard's role in disaster relief and domestic civic action—a relatively low-cost way to generate good will without detracting too greatly from the combat readiness of the standing force. In contrast, intervention for comparable purposes in foreign countries— operations that rely primarily on regulars rather than reservists—fails to provide comparable benefits and detracts from readiness. As a result, the Army is much less amenable to such missions.

For those who advocate expanding the range of tasks that the services will undertake—to encompass, for example, peace operations—military culture is likely to be obstacle. Yet it should be emphasized that to view service peculiarities as entirely negative would be a mistake. Culture provides a source of institutional resilience and character. Service culture figures prominently in the complex web of factors that explain why some men and women choose a career of military service, factors that include an amalgam of patriotism, challenging work, travel, decent pay and benefits, and societal esteem.

No one understands this more clearly than do senior officers. Among this group, awareness of the importance of sustaining service culture tends to be acute. Even if they lack for any other ideas, senior officers can almost always be counted on to protect their service's core beliefs and values. To a large extent, this function defines the standard of institutional good stewardship by which they are judged. Inattention to this requirement invites rebuke, illustrated most recently by the brouhaha over Air Force uniforms. Mortified that their newly redesigned uniforms resulted in their being mistaken for civilian airline pilots, Air Force officers complained mightily, so much so that the newly appointed Chief of Staff made a point of reversing his predecessor's uniform directive within a week of assuming office.

Reservoirs

Several sources from which the Services derive their peculiar cultural traits figure prominently. Among them are: the theories of war and politics that inform the overall thinking of the officer corps; the service's collective reading of the lessons of history (e.g., Vietnam or *Desert Storm*); the service's perception of its own unique contribution to the nations' well being; and the military professional ethic as interpreted by the service. It would not be too far off the mark to say that the chief source of service culture is myth, notions that may make little sense to those who are outside the tribe, but that within the tribe are cherished and carefully passed down from one generation to the next as part of the initiation and socialization process .

All these suggest that service culture is virtually indelible. On occasion in American military history, however, a service has succeeded in recasting its culture in substantially different form, although such change may be painful and does not occur overnight. One example is the Army at the end of the 19th century, an army that had evolved after the Civil War primarily as a constabulary force supporting the continental expansion of the nation. In that capacity, the Army "pacified" the Indians, supported exploration, and provided an important source of engineering expertise needed to exploit the potential of the frontier. By the late 1870s and early 1880s, the days of the constabulary Army were clearly numbered. Recognizing this, visionary senior officers such as William T. Sherman and Emory Upton sounded the call for their service to reinvent itself by shedding its identity as an organization to support internal development and assuming an identify more suited to the times and the likelihood that the United States might become involved in conflict with other nations. Granted, this effort to transform the Army was slow to gain momentum, in no small part because the nation as a whole did not share the viewpoint and concerns of uniformed reformers.

Boosted by the Spanish-American War and its aftermath, however, and benefiting from the visionary political leadership provided by Secretary of War Elihu Root and the sympathetic support of Theodore Roosevelt, this transformation did begin to take hold by the end of the first decade of the 20th century. Although in practice the Army continued to serve in many roles and perform many of the same missions it had in the past, its true and primary reason for existence had become fighting great power wars and its culture changed accordingly.

A second example of significant cultural transformation is found in the Marine Corps during the period between the two world wars. By the time of American entry into World War I, the Marines were known as "State Department troops,"which handled the dirty work of policing the informal American empire in the Caribbean basin. The label carried with it connotations of contempt. For marines, there was little glory and precious little prestige to be gained in serving as the chief instrument of

American power in places like Nicaragua and Haiti, and American entry into World War I did not improve the situation appreciably. During the climactic campaigns of 1918 on the Western Front, the Marine Corps was consigned to a position of embarrassing subordination to the Army—providing a contingent that fought as a brigade within an Army division commanded by Army officers. By the time the war ended, the imperative of redefining the purpose and function of the Marine Corps had become apparent. Failing some such effort and given the scarce number of dollars available for military spending, the case for maintaining the Corps as a separate entity would be difficult to sustain.

As with the Army in the closing decades of the previous century, this prospect of irrelevance inspired a burst of creativity. Shrewdly identifying for itself an essential role within the context of the Navy's abiding preoccupation with a prospective war against Japan, and under the leadership of General John Lejeune, the Marine Corps staked out a new mission for itself as an Advanced Base Force that would secure for the Navy the bases it needed for the conduct of a sustained naval campaign extending across the Pacific. Over the ensuing two decades, this new mission provided the rationale for developing the Fleet Marine Force, a concept that served as the driver for subsequent doctrinal innovation, equipment development, war plans, and exercises. More importantly, the concept also imparted to the Marine Corps a revised sense of purpose and cultural identity it has cherished ever since.

Several conclusions may be drawn from these two examples of profound institutional transformation:

- Services undertake the wrenching process of cultural transformation when necessity compels them to do so. Transformation takes time—years, if not decades—before it truly takes hold.
- Although supportive civilian leadership may play a role, the driving force for transformation is internal; services change themselves.

- Visionary leadership is a prerequisite and is not necessarily easy to find.

Prospects for Change

How susceptible are the military services to comparable cultural change today? Not very. Confidence born of success in the Persian Gulf and unhappy memories that linger from places like Vietnam and Beirut (memories renewed by the experience in Somalia) combine to make the services particularly protective of their established identities and leery of calls to undertake significant change (other than that implied by the continued acquisition of high technology). None of the services faces a true crisis of impending irrelevance that might jolt its leadership into thinking otherwise. This fact should cause would-be military reformers to temper their expectations as to how far present-day American military institutions can be stretched to incorporate nontraditional missions.

However much Americans insist that their military adapt to new circumstances, any wish for change should be done with the understanding that only modest shifts are likely to occur. They may question why the nation's vast military capabilities are so seldom relevant to the actual sources of upheaval in today's world, but they should not expect their queries, objections, or complaints to have more than modest effect. Given the hold of service culture, reinforced by the American experience of the past 25 years, the range of missions to which the services are likely to be amenable will remain limited. No amount of railing against senior officers for their perceived narrow mindedness is likely to change that. Nor is foisting off some new weapon system or demanding changes in doctrine or force structure. Nor will the so called revolution in military affairs provide any near-term remedy.

What, then, can be done to induce the services to undertake a wider menu of missions that might include multilateral peacekeeping or humanitarian relief? Those who would nudge the military toward these sorts of missions need to find ways to reassure service members that such departures from strict orthodoxy do not endanger the status and integrity of their institutions. Accomplishing that requires first persuading Americans to shed unrealistic expectations about the near-term payoff of even the most successful nontraditional military operations. When a Somalia or Rwanda collapses into chaos, military intervention can establish conditions that permit humanitarian operations to proceed, but no military action can restore them as functioning societies. When Haiti falls victim to military thuggery, military action can depose the perpetrators. But military action alone cannot democratize a nation in which few of the prerequisites of democracy exist.

Inducing the services to venture a greater openness and acceptance of nontraditional missions also requires that the American people be disabused to the notion, vastly reinforced by the fabulous success of Desert Storm, that technology is sanitizing war. With rare exceptions, the effective use of force will almost invariably carry with it a substantial risk of American casualties, especially in situations where high technology is of marginal value (e.g., downtown Mogadishu). Indeed, a capacity for absorbing casualties provides one measure of a nation's military capability.

The services may evolve a more accepting attitude toward nontraditional missions if the American public first takes a few modest steps toward desentimentalizing the American soldier. Certainly, the United States should never send its warriors in harm's way without good reason. It should train them well and arm them with the best available equipment. It should honor their sacrifices. It should mourn when they fall in battle. But if policy makers expect the military services to sign up for missions like multilateral peacekeeping or nation building, then the death of American service members cannot be the basis for immediate and automatic recriminations directed at the Services and their leaders, or for precipitous withdrawal that undermines the value of previous sacrifices. By conveying a realistic appreciation of the fact that the use of force entails the likelihood of casualties and that the loss of a single rifleman does not necessarily constitute unacceptable calamity, Americans will encourage the military to evaluate whether or not to embrace nontraditional missions without inordinate anxiety.

Going beyond these modest steps may require resort to more draconian means, efforts relying less on near-term persuasion and more on coercion and (looking to the longer term) wholesale reeducation of the officer corps. Coercion implies assertive civilian control. What steps would reinvigorate civilian control, thereby establishing the preconditions permitting civilian leaders to convince the military to be more receptive to OOTW? First, DOD requires capable civilian leaders with a keen grasp of geopolitics and of the utility and limitations of military power. Second, those civilian leaders need to demonstrate in unmistakable terms that they are in charge. Toward this end, the civilian leadership should insert itself more directly into the process of selecting the senior leadership in each of the services. By rewarding those senior officers who have experience with peace operations, civilian leaders will help insure that their principal military advisers are in sympathy with their view of how to employ force.

Reeducation implies revision of curricula at every level of military education from service academies through war colleges—inculcating into the officer corps a new vision of international politics, a revised understanding of the nature of war, and a new doctrine for the use of force. Reeducation would necessarily extend well beyond the military schoolhouse. It would have to include personnel procedures, those various cues and incentives that determine who gets ahead, who gets the plum assignments, what is viewed as the billet to occupy to get ahead. None of these efforts is likely to have any significant effect unless sustained over an extended period of time.

Am I recommending such a course of action of coercion and reeducation? Emphatically no. Such an effort to assert this sort of civilian control precipitously could well provoke a civil-military crisis. Faced with more intrusive civilian direction, military leaders might turn to the Congress to fend off the importunities of the executive branch, playing off one branch against the other to preserve the status quo. Furthermore, challenging the military's traditional control of officer education and personnel matters in order to force changes in military culture, even if successful, invites problems that at present we may see only dimly. Success in supplanting the military's "warrior" mystic with something more pertinent to missions such as peace enforcement may well lead to the creation of an officer corps that loses its stomach and capacity for more orthodox military operations. In that regard, the experience of nations that have made a career out of peacekeeping (one thinks of Canada) deserves consideration.

7. PEACE OPERATIONS, EMERGENCY LAW ENFORCEMENT, AND CONSTABULARY FORCES

William Rosenau

In recent years, peace operations have been the subject of unprecedented attention, both inside the U.S. Government and within the larger defense policy community. During the past year, for example, the White House issued national-level policy guidance;[1] the Army published a major field manual on the subject;[2] and analysts produced a vast outpouring of studies on peacekeeping, peace enforcement, and related activities. Readiness, training, technology, command and control, and many other dimensions of peace operations have been subjected to this governmental and scholarly focus. One critical aspect of peace operations, public safety, has generally been ignored in policy guidance, doctrine, and scholarly literature. Yet public safety is a particularly demanding and politically sensitive component of U.S. peace operations as diverse as Haiti and Somalia.

William Rosenau is a foreign policy aide in the Senate. He was on the Staff of the CORM and was the special assistant to the Assistant Secretary of Defense for Special Operations and Low Intensity Conflict. He has been associated with the Center for Strategic and International Studies, the Forum for International Policy and the Kennedy School of Government.

During the course of a number of peace operations and other nontraditional military activities, local public safety forces (e.g., police, gendarmeries, and paramilitary forces) have collapsed or been destroyed. In these cases, U.S. military personnel, faced with a law-enforcement vacuum, were compelled to protect civilian lives and property. The U.S. Armed Forces also helped train rudimentary public security or "constabulary" forces capable of maintaining order once American military personnel depart. In each case, however, the U.S. Government was ill prepared to conduct these enforcement and training missions.

Although leaders of the Republican majority in Congress have expressed skepticism about the utility of peace operations[3] and other nontraditional military activities, it is likely that the national interest will require the United States to conduct them during the coming decade. Chaos and instability in Cuba following the collapse of the Castro regime, for example, could lead to a substantial U.S. operation to restore order and promote a democratic transition. Emergency civilian law enforcement and constabulary training are likely to be features of such an operation.

It is unlikely that the United States or its coalition partners will be able to achieve their objectives in an environment that lacks basic law and order. If local public-safety forces are unable or unwilling to provide it, or are politically unacceptable, U.S. forces and their partners will have to assume responsibility. The creation of an effective, relatively humane and non-corrupt constabulary force is another essential ingredient for success. Among other things, such a force will contribute to the prompt departure of American troops, a *sine qua non* for U.S. policy makers in the post-Cold War world. But success in future operations will require changes in the way the U.S. Government, and in particular DOD, plans for and conducts these missions.

After providing some historical background on U.S. public safety assistance during and after the Cold War, this chapter explores roles and missions options that could improve the performance of the United States in overseas enforcement and constabulary training. Particular attention will be paid to the latter, given the political, operational and legal challenges it creates. The chapter will conclude with a discussion of how the proposed changes are likely to conflict with the organizational culture and historical experience of the U.S. Armed Forces.

Cold War Public Safety Assistance

For much of the Cold War, U.S. overseas police training activities focused on the goal of developing bulwarks against Communist expansion in the Third World. Throughout the 1950s and 1960s—the "counterinsurgency era,"[4] in Douglas Blaufarb's phrase—the United States supplied pro-Western regimes with money, equipment and advice in an effort to stem Soviet, Chinese and Cuban-sponsored subversion. According to the tenets of counterinsurgency doctrine, the police, given their supposedly close relationship with the civilian population, were the ideal instrument to serve as the first line of defense against insurgency.

Throughout the 1950s, DOD, the Central Intelligence Agency (CIA), the International Cooperation Agency (the forerunner of AID, the Agency for International Development), and other organizations assisted police and paramilitary forces in the Middle East, Latin America, and Asia, the leading battlegrounds of the Western struggle against communist expansionism. In 1962, in an effort to centralize the U.S. Government's diverse police assistance efforts, the Kennedy administration created the Office of Public Safety (OPS) within AID. At its peak, OPS trained the police forces of 34 nations,[5] both in the field and at the Washington-based International Police Academy, at an annual cost of $60 million dollars.[6] OPS, however, never fit in well with AID's larger mission or organizational culture. Many of that organization's officials viewed the counterinsurgency orientation of OPS as conflicting with the agency's development agenda, and throughout its relatively brief life, OPS remained underfunded and bureaucratically weak. Among other woes, OPS was plagued with the inability to find competent personnel willing to serve abroad for extended periods.[7]

Foreign police and paramilitary training, although nominally centralized in OPS, continued to be conducted by other U.S. agencies, including DOD. A 1970 Army field manual, for instance, describes an expansive role for military police (MP) trainers and advisers in what the service termed "stability operations," (i.e., counterinsurgency). MPs, according to the manual, "are particularly effective in providing advice, training and operational assistance to HC [host country] civil, military and paramilitary police forces in the conduct of countering insurgencies in urban areas."[8] During the 1960s, Army Special Forces (SF) played a significant training role in Latin America; mobile training teams from the 8th SF Group, for example, provided support to paramilitary units throughout South America.[9] Army units also played a constabulary training and civilian law enforcement role during the 1965 invasion of the Dominican Republic (Operation Power Pack), one of the largest peace operations in American history.[10]

Although they conducted law-enforcement related operations, the Armed Forces, like AID, remained institutionally lukewarm to the public safety mission. By the late 1960s, the officer corps had grown increasingly disillusioned with counterinsurgency, which many viewed as a civilian-generated fad that was at best a distraction from the real business of preparing for war. The bitter experience of Vietnam confirmed military suspicions that counterinsurgency was a political tar baby—a high-risk enterprise that typically lacks genuine national commitment and jeopardizes the institutional standing of the defense establishment as a whole.[11] The police training element of counterinsurgency was deemed to be particularly "unsoldierly." Morris Janowitz has placed such antipathy in its historical context:

> The professional soldier resists identifying himself with the 'police,' and the military profession has struggled to distinguish itself from the internal police force . . . . The military tends to

think of police activities as less prestigeful and less honorable tasks, and within the military establishment the military police have had relatively low status.[12]

The military's unease with "nation building," constabulary training and other aspects of counterinsurgency coincided with a major shift in public and congressional attitudes about America's role in the Third World. By the early 1970s, the nation had grown weary of its role as the "world's policeman." "Vietnamization" and the so-called Nixon Doctrine signalled the end of an unlimited U.S. commitment to defend Third World allies. New Left attacks on assistance to repressive U.S. client states fueled congressional concern about American support to undemocratic regimes.

Critics of U.S. assistance to friendly regimes claimed that American personnel were providing torture training to local police, particularly in South America. Such charges were to prove unfounded. As one State Department official condescendingly put it at the time, "no inheritors of the Iberian-Roman tradition seem to need [instruction in torture] from representatives of other cultures."[13] Nevertheless, Congress enacted sweeping changes, and legislation passed during the early 1970s had a major impact on the U.S. Government's law enforcement training activities abroad. The Foreign Assistance Act of 1973 prohibited the use of foreign assistance funds for overseas police training; Section 660 of the Foreign Assistance Act passed the following year, effectively shut down OPS and imposed other restrictions on international law enforcement assistance.[14]

Assistance in the 1980s and 1990s

Following the 1979 Soviet invasion of Afghanistan and other dramatic changes in the international security environment, U.S. national leaders regained a commitment to confronting Soviet challenges in the developing world. The obvious threats to U.S. interests posed by terrorism, insurgency and drug trafficking caused senior policy makers and members of Congress to reevaluate the ban on foreign police training activities. Reagan administration officials argued persuasively that confronting these threats required the U.S. military and other organizations to carry out limited, specialized training of Third World security forces. Congressional waivers and amendments to the Foreign Assistance Act allowed the Departments of State, Defense and Justice to conduct overseas counterdrug and antiterrorism training, as well as the training of national police forces in countries without standing armies, such as Costa Rica and the microstates of the Eastern Caribbean. As of 1990, the U.S. Government was spending a total of $117 million a year to train police forces in 125 countries.[15]

Since its creation in 1986, the Justice Department's International Criminal Investigative Training Assistance Program (ICITAP) has conducted much of U.S. overseas police and criminal-justice system training. Most of this training has focused on developing further the skills of relatively professional police forces in Central America and in the Andes. A direct descendent of OPS, ICITAP has been hampered by many of the problems of its predecessor: the lack of a clear mission; inadequate funding; an inability to deploy quickly and operate with DOD; and poor access to effective personnel. These deficiencies have been apparent in every major contingency operation in which ICITAP has participated. In Panama, for example, one senior U.S. military officer explained how the organization was overwhelmed by its responsibilities: "We tried to push ICITAP in the direction of deploying its people throughout the country to work in every precinct and province . . . .[However, they] could not comprehend operating on this scale."[16] As Richard Shultz has observed, ICITAP, as a new and small organization with a limited mandate, "had never attempted to establish and train an entirely new security force department."[17]

The organization's performance in Somalia was equally inadequate. ICITAP was not configured or funded to provide the type of short-notice constabulary training required in a hostile environment such as Somalia. According to one military observer, ICITAP was plagued by personnel problems: "ICITAP is composed of contract trainers. Many of them take leave from their permanent police jobs or have already retired from the police force. Many are not fit for the [r]igors of austere environments."[18]

In the absence of a civilian agency capable of performing security force training in less-than-permissive environments, the U.S. military has found itself called upon to perform this function. The Armed Forces, however, have done so reluctantly. As suggested earlier, the services have long resisted police-related activities, and in each of the operations cited above, the military performed training operations only after it was clear that no other agency of government could meet the requirements of the mission.

In Panama, the U.S. military created a police training course, and MPs conducted joint patrols with the Panama Public Force, the local constabulary.[19] In Somalia, which had been without a functioning criminal justice system for years, "facilitating the restoration of a police force (within legal parameters) and a judicial system was a requirement and a challenge," according to one Army study.[20] Marines in Mogadishu and other parts of the country trained and helped support what they termed "auxiliary security forces" to carry out rudimentary law enforcement activities, such as protecting lives and property of both Somalis and foreigners.[21] Most recently, in Cap-Haitien, Limbé, and other provincial Haitian towns, Army SF were involved in establishing new constabulary forces after the Haitian military (known as the FAd'H) disbanded in the aftermath of the U.S. invasion.[22] It is clear that such activities occupy a legal gray area, given Section 660 restrictions.[23] But it is also clear that no nonmilitary institution was capable of performing this essential task.

Emergency Law Enforcement

The Armed Forces have also been called upon to perform short-term emergency law enforcement during peace operations and other military activities where host nation civilian authorities were inadequate or had collapsed outright. Under the law of land warfare, military commanders have an obligation to ensure, as far as possible, "public order and safety"—but only if the United States is an "occupying power."[24] During Haiti, Somalia and other operations, however, the United States did not consider itself as such, and so did not have any formal responsibilities in this area. As with constabulary training, the military accepted this function reluctantly and only after it was clear that no other U.S. or foreign agency was capable of performing it. In a number of cases, however, the reluctance of the U.S. Government, including the military, to plan for or to carry out this responsibility has created political problems and potentially jeopardized the overall success of the mission. This is a demonstration of the principle that, in the environment short of war, tactical actions can have profound operational and even strategic consequences.

In Panama, for example, U.S. military and civilian officials were unprepared for the widespread looting and other disorder that broke out following the invasion. At the very least, the chaos threatened an orderly transition from Noriega-style praetorianism to democracy. More recently, during the first days of the Haiti operation, senior military and civilian officials indicated that U.S. forces would not conduct law enforcement operations. Undersecretary of Defense for Policy Walter Slocombe told the House Armed Services Committee that U.S. forces would assure "essential civic order," but they would not "take over general policing."[25]

But as the United States discovered, the Haitian forces responsible for maintaining order were the same thuggish element that had terrorized the population for decades. Because they had been told to leave law enforcement to indigenous forces, U.S. troops stood by while the FAd'H beat to death exuberant but nonviolent protesters in Port-au-Prince.[26] Worldwide television coverage and the resulting outcry in the United States forced a revision in the rules of engagement to allow greater military protection for the Haitian population. Although it probably did not cause long-term damage to U.S. policy, the image of U.S.

forces standing by while civilians were beaten did tarnish an otherwise exemplary operation and call into question (at least for some observers) America's commitment to a democratic transition.

Roles and Missions Options

Ever since the public disorder that followed the invasion of Panama, senior officials within the Department of Defense have recognized that gaps in capabilities exist with respect to emergency law enforcement and constabulary training. ICITAP has been subject to particular criticism in the department. While there are some indications that ICITAP's performance in Haiti may be an improvement over its earlier efforts in Somalia and Panama, other signs suggest continuing organizational problems.[27] ICITAP officials have made it clear that they believe the agency must be reorganized to make it more interoperable with DOD and other government departments with national security responsibilities. [28]

There is a dilemma of sorts at play here. Clearly reform is required, but given bureaucratic, budgetary and cultural realities, it appears unlikely that ICITAP will be reformed substantially anytime soon. At present, ICITAP lacks the command and control, accountability, and the ability to deploy quickly and operate effectively in rigorous environments. The Federal Bureau of Investigation and a small handful of other non-DOD agencies possess some of these essentially martial characteristics. However, it is probably unrealistic to expect civilian entities to perform as well as the Armed Forces do in short-notice operations in hostile environments. The U.S. Armed Forces, after all, have organized, trained and equipped themselves for this mission since the earliest days of the Republic. Thus, although the mission properly belongs to other agencies, the Armed Forces may be the best choice for carrying it out.

Although the United Nations has become increasingly involved in constabulary training and has played a significant postconflict role in countries like Cambodia and El Salvador, it has done so with mixed success. The United Nations has recognized the importance of law enforcement in the context of traditional peacekeeping operations, and as a result, it may expand its training capabilities. But the ability of the United Nations to carry out constabulary training during an insurgency, civil war, or other less-than-permissive environment is very much in doubt, given its past performance in places like Somalia. A U.S. military officer with extensive MP experience in Somalia offered the following assessment of the UN's performance:

> The UN is not equipped or motivated to quickly support us. They proved it in Somalia. They are too bureaucratic to get anything done. Additionally, their agenda may not correspond to our mission. Their personnel most likely will not have the expertise . . . to accomplish the mission. I found their police advisors (both military and civilian) to be there for the money; mission accomplishment was not a priority.[29]

And although U.S. coalition partners (particularly Britain and Canada) have carried out constabulary training in recent peace operations, the interests of the United States and its friends may not always coincide. As a result, we may not always be able to rely on them to provide more than ancillary training support. One could also argue that private contractors might be able to supply training and support. During the 1950s, for instance, Sea Systems, a private U.S. firm, trained and supplied Royal Thai paramilitary police forces. [30] However, contract personnel, like foreign governments, could conclude that participating in any give peace operation or other activity is not in their interest.

As a result, U.S. military commanders, as they prepare for the next significant peace operation or related contingency activity, are likely to confront the same law-enforcement and constabulary training difficulties faced by their predecessors. Regrettably, other agencies of government with responsibilities in the environment short of war, including AID and the Departments of

State and Justice, cannot be counted on to perform in austere, demanding environments, particularly on short notice. With the exception of the State Department, these agencies have never seen themselves as instruments of U.S. national security policy; rather, they exist to serve domestic constituencies.

The Department of Defense should first accept the fact that U.S. military forces have conducted emergency law enforcement and constabulary training in the past and are likely to do so in the future. (Interestingly, the British Army has acknowledged that the military has responsibility for ensuring that local security forces can maintain order during peace operations.[31]) Military planners and civilian national security officials also need to acknowledge that during time-urgent operations that take place in hostile environments, there is no effective alternative to the U.S. military performing these missions.

By the same token, however, the Congress and other institutions must recognize that an open-ended obligation for the Armed Forces to conduct emergency law enforcement and constabulary training would be a serious misuse of defense resources. ICITAP and other civilian agencies, while deficient in short-term, quick-response training in demanding environments, can conduct effective medium- and long-term constabulary training. Further reforms planned within ICITAP,[32] combined with vigorous preconflict efforts to encourage allied participation in training, should reduce the temptation to dump all the burdens of this mission on the military.

Given the Army's significant military police capabilities, it is appropriate to assign it lead responsibility for maintaining public order during significant military operations.[33] Throughout its history, Army personnel have controlled crowds, conducted police-like patrols, trained indigenous security forces, and carried out other overseas law-enforcement missions. When appropriate, Marine Corps forces (or other service personnel) could be called upon to perform this function, as they did during Operation *Restore Hope* in Somalia. The Army would also be given responsibility for conducting short-term foreign security-force training. Military police, supported by appropriate special operations forces (i.e., SF,[34] civil affairs and psychological operations units) and allied/coalition personnel would carry out the training and support. These activities would include combined U.S.-host nation joint patrols and other operations to ensure the creation of a professional force that supports U.S. policy goals and values, including human rights. Support could also include the provision of vehicles, weapons and other equipment, and the reconstruction and repair of law-enforcement facilities as required.

U.S. military responsibility for this training would be limited to a 6-month period. Longer-term training and reconstitution would remain the responsibility of ICITAP. Broader efforts aimed at creating or reestablishing a functioning criminal justice system would remain within the ken of civilian agencies, including ICITAP. When and where appropriate, however, special operations forces and other military personnel could participate on an *ad hoc* basis. The Army could also conduct specialized training for reserve units that might be called upon to perform the constabulary training mission. Finally, the Army would continue to develop doctrine for this function. A recent draft field manual, for example, outlines the ways in which MP operations can contribute to U.S. goals in the environment short of war by training, equipping, and supporting indigenous paramilitary and civilian police agencies.[35]

Toward this end, two steps need to be taken. First, the Secretary of Defense should revise DOD Directive 5100.1, which governs service roles and functions. Second, the Congress should hold hearings to consider the elimination of legal restrictions on constabulary force training by DOD personnel. Section 660 of the Foreign Assistance Act, for example, was created in the aftermath of abuses that allegedly took place during the Cold War. Given the widespread recognition that in the post-Cold War world, the US military can be an instrument for building democratic institutions in the developing world,[36] it is appropriate to ask whether these restrictions continue to serve US national security interests.

Finally, it is worth adding that none of the proposals outlined above would *compel* the National Command Authority (i.e., the President and the Secretary of Defense, or their duly deputized alternates or successors) to use military forces to conduct emergency law enforcement or constabulary training. In relatively benign environments, or in instances in which actions by the Armed Forces would have negative political consequences for the United States, civilian agencies would be more appropriate instruments. In such cases, the President should have the flexibility to employ nonmilitary organizations.

Sources of Opposition

An expanded role for the U.S. military is likely to meet with congressional and executive branch opposition. Within the Congress, there is a widespread feeling that the Armed Forces have been overly involved with UN-sponsored peace operations and other nontraditional military activities. As a result, members of Congress, particularly within the Republican Party, are likely to resist a formalized DOD role in emergency law enforcement and constabulary training.[37] Within the executive branch, some State and Justice Department officials who have a stake in current organizational arrangements are likely to oppose any measures that reduce their policy oversight and administrative involvement.

The most significant opposition, however, is likely to come from within DOD itself. This is ironic, given that a number of defense organizations have recognized the need for changes in the way the United States conducts emergency law enforcement and training. The Department of the Army, for example, currently is supporting a more formal and vigorous service role in overseas law enforcement and constabulary training.[38] But some elements of the officer corps are remain profoundly troubled by these tasks. Some of the concern is focused on readiness, and the belief that nontraditional missions will "dull the warrior edge" of the Armed Forces, thus hampering their ability to defend the nation's vital interests in wartime. Other critics worry that DOD will become a "'cash cow'"for civilian agencies unable or unwilling to pay for nation assistance, peacekeeping and other activities out of their own budgets. However, the most sustained attacks on greater military involvement in overseas emergency law enforcement and constabulary training will come from officers who are not concerned with readiness and budgets *per se*. Rather, these individuals are likely to derive their criticisms from an institutional view of the proper role of the military that is sharply opposed to most noncombat activities.

As suggested above, successful peace operations and other nontraditional military missions are likely to require adequate preparation for emergency law enforcement and training. But for a number of analysts, senior officers, and statesmen, the Armed Forces exist primarily, if not exclusively, for the purpose of fighting and winning the nation's wars. General Colin Powell and former Defense Secretary Caspar Weinberger are two of the better known exponents of this view. A cruder example can be found in a recent Heritage Foundation publication, in which a critic of nontraditional military missions argued, "There is no other reason for the Pentagon to exist except to organize, outfit, and train combat troops to prevail in battle over America's enemies."[39]

For much of its existence before the Cold War, however, the U.S. military, and the Army in particular, conducted a variety of noncombat missions that are today labeled "nontraditional" or "operations other than war." Public works and riot control at home and nation-building activities abroad were part of a portfolio of tasks imposed upon the Armed Forces, which conceived of themselves as more than just the nation's warfighters. In Samuel Huntington's memorable phrase, the Army saw itself as the "general servant"[40] of the state capable of performing virtually any task required of it by civilian leaders.

Victory over the Axis powers in World War II, the demands created by the global Soviet challenge, and the national and institutional agonies generated by the Vietnam War helped create and sustain an organizational vision quite different from the one described above. This vision, which reached fruition during the Gulf War, holds as its central tenet the belief that the Armed Forces exist solely to fight and win the nation's wars. Not every conflict can be considered a war, however. The American officer corps, as described by A.J. Bacevich, tends to see "true" war as a relatively short-duration contest between warriors that is fought to achieve unambiguous military and political objectives. [41] Other forms of conflict, as well as noncombat military activities, frequently are derided as distractions at best and at worse a threat to the institution's ability to prepare for "real" war, its *raison d'être*.

Since the collapse of the Soviet empire, however, the U.S. military has found itself increasingly called upon to perform nonwarfighting missions, particularly in the Third World periphery. This is an ironic outcome for the officer corps. For many professional soldiers, the great victory over Saddam Hussein was the culmination of their 20-year effort to exorcise counterinsurgency, low-intensity conflict, and other Vietnam-era demons from the U.S. military repertoire. The crushing triumph over Iraq seemed to auger a new generation of warfare characterized by speed, high technology, and minimal U.S. casualties.

But as the U.S. military discovered in Somalia and Haiti, not all conflicts resemble the technology-intensive, short-duration conventional warfare that took place in the Persian Gulf. Unrealistic expectations about future conflicts in which American miliary power might be brought to bear are likely to present major impediments to U.S. success against state and nonstate actors adversaries who employ techniques such as terrorism, subversion, and insurgency.[42] Although well-trained general purpose forces can perform well in nonwarfighting missions, some specialized skills are required. More important, nonmilitary agencies of government need to have their capabilities upgraded; given the heavily political environment in which these operations take place, it is crucial that the Departments of State and Justice,

AID, and other organizations be able to perform as part of an interagency team.[43]

Conclusion

As a number of analysts have observed, the well-defined "Chinese wall" that existed between civilian and military functions during the Cold War has eroded significantly. Martin Edmonds observes, "The usual distinction between armed services and such state organizations as the police and internal security agencies is no longer as clear-cut and well-defined as before."[44] A number of the factors contributing to this trend have already been discussed. One other contributing element bears mentioning. *The United States and its allies*, no longer faced with a Soviet superpower and the threat of nuclear Armageddon, now *has* the "luxury" of using military instruments to address what had earlier been considered to be serious, but essentially nonmilitary problems,e.g., drug trafficking, illegal migration, and humanitarian disasters.

For some observers, the erosion of the Chinese wall has dire consequences for the American Republic. Charles Dunlap, for example, in his apocalyptic satire, "The Origins of the American Military Coup of 2012," suggests that greater military involvement in activities such as law enforcement will have the pernicious effect of injecting the Armed Forces into domestic politics.[45] Congress and the American public, however, are more ambiguous in their approach to the issue of how the military should be employed to perform tasks other than fighting and winning the nation's wars. There is a clear resistance to having U.S. forces embroiled in some nontraditional missions, particularly when they are carried out under UN auspices, such as the UNOSOM II operation in Somalia. It is also clear that they believe the Armed Forces have a problem-solving utility that goes beyond warfighting. As domestic problems grow, and ethnic conflict and other forms of instability continue to rage abroad, U.S. military leaders may be compelled to justify the nation's $250 billion per year defense budget on some nonwarfighting grounds.

What this suggests is that nonwarfighting activities may become less and less alien, and more and more attractive in the future. This is not to argue that professional soldiers should embark on a cynical search for relevance and self-justification. Rather, the officer corps, particularly in the Army, should explore how these missions might contribute to a new, post-Cold War organizational vision for the military.[46] Such a vision could serve as the starting point for more robust and effective U.S. responses to the challenges posed by peace operations and other elements of the environment short of war.

Notes

1. "The Clinton Administration's Policy on Reforming Multilateral Peace Operations," The White House, Washington, DC, May 1994, 1-15. This is the unclassified version of Presidential Decision Directive 25 (PDD-25), the administration's most important policy document on the subject.

2. Department of the Army, *FM 100-23: Peace Operations* (Washington, DC: Headquarters, Department of the Army, December 1994).

3. For example, see David C. Morrison, "Republicans at War With Peacekeeping," *National Journal*, 11 March 1995, 615.

4. Douglas S. Blaufarb, Douglas S. *The Counterinsurgency Era: US Doctrine and Performance* (New York: The Free Press, 1977).

5. Comptroller General of the United States. U.S. General Accounting Office Report to the Congress, "Stopping U.S. Assistance to Foreign Police and Prisons," 19 February 1976, 10.

6. Vietnam, of course, was the focus of much of the U.S. Government's training efforts during the 1960s and early 1970s. For example, Blaufarb notes that the CIA trained the Police Special Branch in Saigon. Blaufarb, 212.

7. Thomas Lobe, "The Rise and Decline of the Office of Public Safety", *Armed Forces and Society* 9, no. 2 (Winter 1983): 187-123. A somewhat more sympathetic overview of OPS can be found in Lefever, Ernest W. *U.S. Public Safety Assistance: An Assessment*, report prepared for the U.S. Agency for International Development (The Brookings Institution, Washington, DC, February 1970), 124-150.

8. Department of the Army. *FM19-50: Military Police in Stability Operations* Washington, DC: Headquarters, Department of the Army, February 1970, II-4.

9. 8th SF Group, 1st SF, "Special Action Force for Latin America: 1966 Historical Supplement," Fort Gulick, Panama, 1966, unpaginated.

10. This aspect of Power Pack remains obscure. For a useful discussion, see Linda Flanagan, "Case Study: The Dominican Intervention of 1965," study prepared for the Commission on Roles and Missions of the Armed Forces, Department of Defense, Washington, DC, 25 January 1995, 7-13.

11. Carnes Lord, "American Strategic Culture in Small Wars," *Small Wars and Insurgencies* 3, no. 3 (Winter 1992): 211.

12. Morris Janowitz, *The Professional Soldier* (New York: The Free Press, 1971). A discussion of the Army's institutional resistance to counterinsurgency can be found in Andrew Bacevich, The Army in Vietnam (Baltimore: The Johns Hopkins University Press, 1986).

13. As quoted in Lefever, 94.

14. U.S. General Accounting Office, "Foreign Aid: Police Training and Assistance," report to congressional requesters, March 1992, 2.

15. Ibid., 3.

16. Richard H. Shutz, Jr., *In the Aftermath of War: US Support for Reconstruction and Nation-Building in Panama Following Just Cause* (Maxwell Air Force Base, Alabama: Air University Press, August 1993), 51.

17. Ibid., 49.

18. Memorandum for COL Gregson from LTC Stephen M. Spataro, 705th Military Police Battalion, Fort Leavenworth, Kansas, "Constabulary Forces," 27 December 1994, 3.

19. For a description of these activities, see Shultz, 45-54; memorandum for commander in chief, US Southern Command, from US Special Operations Command, "Organization of Nation Building Forces," 8 January 1990, unpaginated; and Colonel Alexander M. Walczak, "Conflict Termination—Transitioning from Warrior to Constable, A Primer," Study Project (Carlisle Barracks, PA: U.S. Army War College, 1992), 14-17.

20. "Operation *Restore Hope* Lessons Learned Report (3 December 92-4 May 93)" Center for Army Lessons Learned, US Army Combined Arms Command, Ft. Leavenworth, Kansas, n.d., XIV-39.

21. Jonathan T. Dworken, *Operation Restore Hope: Preparing and Planning the Transition to UN Operations* (Alexandria, VA: Center for Naval Analyses, March 1994), 25. It is worth noting that this was not the US government's first experience with police training in Somalia. The Civil Police Administration, OPS's predecessor organization, began training and other support to the Somali National Police as early as 1958. A.A. Castagno, "The Somali National Police and AID Assistance'," n.p., n.d. (Stanford Research Institute, 1969?), 1.

22. John F. Harris, "Haitians Jeer U.S. Sponsored Policemen," *Washington Post,* 10 October 1994, A14, and Bob Shacochis, "The Immaculate Invasion," *Harper's*, February 1995, 44. The FAd'H (i.e., the Haitian Armed Forces) was the acronym applied collectively to the army, navy, police and other "public safety" forces.

23. Memorandum to Commander, Unified Task Force, from F. M. Lorenz, Office of the Staff Judge Advocate, Unified Task Force Somalia,"Operation Restore Hope After Action Report/Lessons Learned," Unclassified, n.d., 36.

24. Department of the Army Field Manual, *FM27-10: The Law of Land Warfare* (Washington, DC: Headquarters, Department of the Army July 1956), 141.

25. "Hearing of the House Armed Services Committee, Haiti Situation," Federal News Service transcript, 7 October 1994, 6.

26. Douglas Farah, "Haitian Police Attack Crowd; US Troops Watch," *Washington Post*, 21 September 1994, 1.

27. See for a sharply critical view on ICITAP's performance in Haiti, see Memorandum for Janet Reno, Attorney General, from R. John Theriault, Jr., "Director's Report on ICITAP," 28 February 1995, 2.

28. Author's interviews with senior ICITAP officials, Washington DC, 16 March 1995.

29. Memorandum for COL Gregson from LTC Stephen M. Spataro, 2.

30. Thomas Lobe, *U.S. National Security Policy and Aid to the Thailand Police*, Monograph Series in World Affairs, Graduate School of International Studies, University of Denver, 1977, 23

31. British Army, *Wider Peacekeeping*, Field Manual (Fourth Draft), n.p., n.d. [1994], 3-14.

32. According to senior officials in the agency, an effort is underway within ICITAP and the Department of Justice to improve its capabilities in the post-conflict environment. Author's interview with ICITAP

officials, Washington, DC, 16 March 1995.

33. Technically speaking, the armed services do not conduct operations; rather, they organize, train and equip forces which are provided to the regional commanders-in-chief who actually carry them out.

34. Support to constabulary training could be included as part of the Special Forces' foreign internal defense (FID) mission area--broadly speaking, government-to-government programs "designed to free and protect a nation from lawlessness, subversion, and insurgency by emphasizing the building of viable institutions that respond to the needs of society." Joint Chiefs of Staff, *Joint Tactics, Techniques and Procedures for Foreign Internal Defense*, Joint Publication 3-07.1, 20 December 1993, I-1.

35. Department of the Army. *Military Police Support to Operations Other Than War*. draft field manual, n.p., n.d. [Washington, DC, 1994?], sec. 4-5 (c).

36. This is implied, for example, in A National Security Strategy of Engagement and Enlargement (Washington, DC: The White House, February 1995), 1-32.

37. See for example Major Garrett, "Military's New Role Criticized," *Washington Times*, 4 October 1994, A16.

38. This can found in a Department of the Army-sponsored report, *The 21st Century Army: Roles, Missions and Functions in an Age of Information and Uncertainty* (Ann Arbor, MI: Vector Research, Inc., n.d. [1995]), 51.

39. Thomas P. Sheehy, "No More Somalias: Reconsidering Clinton's Doctrine of Military Humanitarianism," Heritage Foundation *Backgrounder*, 20 December 1993, 12.

40. Samuel P. Huntington, *The Soldier and the State* (Cambridge, MA: Harvard University Press, Belknap Press, 1957), 261.

41. A. J. Bacevich, "Use of Force in Our Time, " *Wilson Quarterly* 19, no. 1 (Winter 1995): 57.

42. A useful discussion of the tension between peace operations and the military's dominant warfighting culture can be found in Martin P. Adams, "Peace Enforcement Versus American Strategic Culture," *Strategic Review* 23, no. 1 (Winter 1995): 21.

43. Ideas for reforming the interagency process can be found in Office of the Assistant Secretary of Defense (Special Operations/Low-Intensity Conflict), "Peacetime Engagement: A Policy for the Environment Short of War," working paper, draft 5, unclassified, 14

April 1993, 13-15.

44. Martin Edmonds, *Armed Services and Society*, IUS Special Editions on Armed Forces and Society, No. 2 (Boulder, CO: Westview Press, 1990, 25.

45. Charles J. Dunlap, Jr. "The Origins of the American Military Coup of 2012," *Parameters* 22, no. 1 (Winter 1992/93): 4. For a different view, see William Rosenau, "Non-Traditional Missions and the Future of the U.S. Military," *Fletcher Forum of World Affairs* 18, no. 1 (Winter/Spring 1994): 31-48.

46. This idea is drawn from John K. Setear, et al., The Army in a Changing World: The Role of Organizational Vision (Santa Monica, CA: The Rand Corporation, June 1990), 67; and Carl H. Builder, The Masks of War: American Military Styles in Strategy and Analysis (Baltimore, MD: Johns Hopkins University Press, 1989), 185-193.

8. CONTRACTING AND PRIVATIZATION IN PEACE OPERATIONS

Christine Cervenak and George T. Raach

Much has been written about the advantages of privatization and contracting by the government. Contracting for goods and services is as old as the Republic, and the present trend is to do more rather than less. Although we often think of contracting as more appropriate for military peacetime administrative and housekeeping activities, it can have value in peace operations as well. Under some circumstances, contracting out can preserve readiness and permit military forces to concentrate on their core competencies without dissipating resources. Contractors provided support to U.S. forces in Somalia, Rwanda, and Haiti. For example, figures provided to the Commission by the Department of Defense Comptroller show that about 30 percent

Christine M. Cervenak is an international lawyer with extensive experience with U.N. operations in Central America and the Middle East. From 1987 to 1990 Ms. Cervenak was an attorney-advisor in the Office of the Legal Advisor, U.S. Department of State. She is a former Visiting Fellow at the Human Rights Program at Harvard Law School.

George T. Raach, a retired Army officer, is a member of the CORM's professional staff. He has been the Military Assistant to the Deputy Under Secretary of Defense for Policy, the staff director for the DOD report to Congress on the Persian Gulf War, and a member of the faculties at the Army, Navy, and National War Colleges.

of the total costs for operations in Somalia were for contract expenses, primarily logistics and facility construction. Although there is much information available with respect to "conventional" contracting, contracting by the U.S. Government for requirements specific to peace operations is still relatively new. While many of the general government contracting principles apply in the context of peace operations, there are differences that must be considered. Given the wide range of activities involved, this chapter focuses on the issue of outsourcing or contracting out of activities specifically relevant to peace operations and draws some general conclusions about contracting that apply to any peace operation. Many of the macroeconomic issues related to outsourcing (e.g., effect on tax revenues, on job creation, and on private investment) are beyond the scope of this chapter, although these issues merit consideration during the decisionmaking and contract writing processes.[1]

Why contract out in the first place? Outsourcing offers a number of interrelated features to planners concerned with finding ways to provide needed capabilities without overextending the force. Under some circumstances, contracting may offer cost efficiencies that make operations cheaper than using government resources. Or, contracting may be needed to preserve government-owned assets as a hedge against unforeseen contingencies or conflicts. It may also offer a method for providing goods and services required in excess of the government's capacity to provide them. In this sense, contracting may solve a problem created by a large, unpredicted requirement because contractors may be able to provide goods and services more rapidly than the government. Finally, in some cases, contracting out permits the government the latitude of not spending money to maintain seldom-used, noncritical capabilities readily available on the open market.

Contracting and Government Capacity

Regardless of the reason, contracting can have positive ramifications for the government's capacity to conduct peace operations and to simultaneously meet other national security requirements. Contracting may be advantageous where it supplements government activities whose resources may be needed elsewhere. For example, earlier chapters highlight the fact that forces engaged in peace operations and the resources to support them are not immediately available for use in conventional combat operations. This occurs not because peace operations per se undermine the ability of the force to perform combat missions, but because of the distances over which forces must be transported from one operation to another, the assets required for transportation, and where appropriate, the need to reequip and provide refresher training make rapid redeployment problematic. Also, some capabilities are available to a limited extent in existing force structures. These include such critical support activities as those conducted by, *inter alia,* engineer construction units required to build bases and improve roadways, water purification detachments, various types of transportation companies, and port operating units. If they are committed in one operation, they will not be available for another.

These types of units and others will be required in the early stages of any crisis response deployment—to include crises requiring conventional combat capabilities and some peace operations where the initial environment may be nonpermissive. However, in peace operations, it may be possible to replace certain military units with contractors as the situation stabilizes and levels of consent to the presence of the force increase.

Thus, contracting may also serve as a sort of "take-out mechanism." In some cases military personnel and resources are needed to begin the job, but contractors may complete it.[2] For example, military personnel may establish and operate water purification points initially, as was the case in Rwanda, but contractors may be commissioned to take over that function when appropriate. Another example is the construction of military barracks, which if done by contractors, frees military engineering assets for other activities. Rotating activities from the military to the civilian sector under appropriate circumstances can make military units available for potential conventional conflict without disrupting ongoing peace operations. This is an important consideration since, presumably, peace operations will be conducted only in areas where the U.S. has significant interests. Thus, precipitous withdrawal or termination of the operation could result in a much larger conflict that would undermine American goals and objectives.

If we accept the conclusion that outsourcing can offer positive benefits, both for ongoing peace operations and for the capability to perform conventional military operations by "freeing up" military capacity, then it is necessary to determine what sorts of activities are candidates for outsourcing. It is not difficult to construct a specific list of candidate activities; however, such candidates are appropriate for contracting depending on the type of operation and the environment in which it is likely to occur.

It is more useful to determine the general types of governmental capacities along a spectrum that suggests whether contracting for such capabilities would be appropriate. The spectrum of U.S. Government capacity includes four general categories:

- Activities that the government now has the capacity to implement and should continue to do so. Among these are combat operations such as forced entry and operations that are so sensitive that close government control is required (e.g., psychological operations or implementation of deception plans).
- Activities and functions for which the government does not have current capacity, but for which it should develop capacity to some degree and maintain control of the development process. These capacities include, for example, providing effective counter measures—in terms of both

equipment and doctrine—for new weapons or techniques developed by potential adversaries.

● Activities for which the government does not have, and for which there is no need to develop, capacity. This area includes functions often performed by various private volunteer organizations (PVOs) or nongovernmental organizations (NGOs), such as the management of orphanages to care for children whose parents have become victims of a conflict.

● The activities of most interest here include those for which the government may have a capacity, but which may be accomplished by contractors equally well and perhaps with more overall efficiency under certain circumstances. Examples include truck transport in benign environments, longer term public safety support functions, operation of refugee camps, and the construction of facilities to support operating forces such as barracks and warehouses. It should be noted that including an activity as a candidate for contracting does not mean that the government ought to divest itself of that capability for the future. This, in fact, is one of the disadvantages to contracting, as will be discussed further.

Along this spectrum, one can see that contracting is beneficial when it adds to the capacity to carry out necessary activities the U.S. Government need not, or cannot,[3] undertake itself. Personnel and materiel resources are thus preserved, and gaps in capabilities are filled. Usually, contracting will be limited to clearly noncombat activities such as logistics support. However, contracting may cross into the gray area bordering on combat, such as providing security for installations or creating and advising local police forces. Contracting, however, does not relieve the military of its requirements to retain critical capabilities. For example, the United States will always have a requirement to move personnel and materiel around an area of operations. Sometimes, contractors can fulfill that requirement. On other occasions the military must provide it because the operational environment in terms of enemy activity, geography, or weather requires military performance or because the military can begin doing it earlier than contractors. Thus, while contracting may make sense under some circumstances (because it conserves military transportation assets that may be needed elsewhere), the military must always retain a transport capability. In short, unlike privatization of other activities that effectively relieves the government of the capacity to perform that function in the future (privatization of maintenance depots, for example), contracting in peace operations is a matter of preservation of resources and convenience.

Contracting can have negative consequences as well as positive ones. Clearly, activities that are inappropriate for the private sector fall into this category, such as combat or the direct support of forces engaged in combat.[4] Also, there are situations where the United States needs to build or maintain capacity for strategic or other important reasons, and contracting-out may prevent it from doing so. That, in fact, is one of the disadvantages of contracting if officials allow some capabilities to atrophy because contracting seems to work well enough. For example, if the government does not have adequate capacity to detect and remove certain types of land mines, contracting this activity to a private firm fills a "gap" in some situations[5]. Yet outsourcing may damage U.S. capability to perform this function under other circumstances if, because of heavy reliance on contractors, military specialists are denied training opportunities, or if appropriate equipment is not developed and procured.[6] Thus, a certain amount of caution is warranted so that the military capability to perform certain critical skills is not undermined by short-term expediency.

Contract Timing

Contracting, in general, is more appropriate for activities that are less urgent, since the contracting process is typically time consuming. Contracting may be disadvantageous if it is unable to meet an urgent timetable, such as during contingency operations that occur with little or no warning and require a rapid response. In many circumstances, however, a lengthy process may be made more expeditious with standby or retainer contracts. Although one pays for the standby capacity, the practice often makes sense. The Army, for example, maintains a retainer arrangement with Brown and Root, Inc., a large engineering firm. In exchange for the retainer fee, Brown and Root conducts engineering studies of areas for which the Army has an operational interest and agrees to take on certain functions on a cost-plus basis during emergencies. This arrangement, called LOGCAP, proved its worth during operations in Somalia, Rwanda, and Haiti where Brown and Root was able to expeditiously provide base construction, logistics, and other services.

Another factor that must be kept in mind when considering the need for timeliness is that contracts are not always sufficiently flexible (i.e., responsive to unexpected changes) to be appropriate in the peace operations context. In short, contracts rarely take into account of all possible contingencies caused by changes on the ground in the area of operation, or by changes to the mandate. Changes of this type may require midcourse contract modifications and time-consuming renegotiation, which, in turn, can engender critical delays in performance. Time-sensitive activities may suffer also to the extent that contractors who are unable or unwilling to perform to specification cannot be replaced rapidly (because of lack of alternative contractors with similar capabilities or other factors).[7] Other problems delaying contract performance and flexibility may include labor shortages, work stoppages, strikes, or other labor problems.[8]

Cost Efficiency

Under some circumstances, contracting can be more cost efficient than using government resources. For example, as mentioned earlier, even though contracting for a capability may be costly in the short run, that may be a more efficient course of action if it preserves scarce or more expensive government-owned assets for other, high-priority operations. The idea that contracting may be more cost efficient than performing an activity in-house is derived from the assumption that generally, profit seekers are more motivated to "eliminate random inefficiencies," enforce cost discipline, and accelerate innovation.[9] Theoretically, at least, some of the savings generated in this manner are passed on to the government in the form of lower contracting costs.

Often this is precisely what occurs. However, in other cases, even when it appears that contracting might save money as a result of more efficient management, that perception may be wrong. This might be the case if there is a lack of sufficient competition in the market place with respect to a particular capability.[10] Where there is insufficient competition, costs may be higher, since one or two contractors can more or less determine their charges independent of market pressures. Another obstacle to reduced costs involves the government's supervision of the contract. If governmental oversight is itself costly, inadequate, or both, then cost efficiencies are likely to be slim.[11] Contract oversight extends beyond monitoring work in progress, which may be the easiest part of the equation, and includes establishing initial requirements, reviewing proposals, negotiating, and writing the contract itself. Inadequate governmental management of the contracting process may lead to poorly written contracts, which include gaps and ambiguities that, in turn, may then lead to governmental vulnerability to higher costs and, from the government's perspective, substandard performance.

Political Considerations:
Control and Contract Performance

John Donahue argues that contracting out is appropriate where the end result is more important than the means; it is inappropriate where the means is more important than the ends.[12]

This distinction suggests various costs and benefits associated with the contractor's performance. In other words, contractors are a good mechanism for achieving public goals when they are allowed to do what they do best: find innovative, cost-efficient ways to achieve those goals. However, contractors may be an inappropriate vehicle for achieving governmental ends when the specific actions for achieving such ends are very important, unpredictable, and/or politically sensitive.

Consider a classic example of a task where the means are important and where contracting may be inappropriate: the protection of the President. A contractor for this task would likely try to minimize costs by, for instance, restricting crowds to a mile away from the President, having the President travel incognito, or limiting public appearances.[13] These restrictions on the President's activities may cut costs but are likely to interfere with the way the President works, and so are unacceptable. Although one could draft a contract describing the work of the Secret Service, the contractor would have to be so flexible and so subordinate to the desires of the White House in contract performance that it ultimately would look like a government entity and costs would be relatively high.

Another particularly poignant example more closely related to peace operations in which "means matter" involves contracts where contractors are performing police or security functions with the potential for the use of deadly or injurious force. Although the benefits fall primarily in the areas of increased governmental capability and possibly monetary savings, the potential downsides to contracting such functions, depending on the situation, are serious. These include: the lack of complete control of training, lack of accountability for every action, and possible ramifications for broader U.S. goals; the perception/reality that the contractor is a U.S. agent and therefore the U.S. assumes symbolic, political, and legal liability for the contractor's use of force; and the lack of flexibility in controlling performance in light of unforeseen developments (e.g., where the threat of armed attack or resistance is not easily predictable).[14]

Failure of contracted public safety forces to act responsibly can have dramatic effects on the degree of acceptance of the peace operation by the local population and, ultimately, on overall success.

As discussed previously in this chapter, contractors are viewed as having tendencies toward innovation and efficiency in performing a task. The contract seems to imply that the government consents to these tendencies as long as there are no provisions to the contrary. Although contracts may stipulate that performance be by individuals with specific qualifications and training, such requirements are not always adequate to control all critical aspects of actual performance. Because most work requirements in peace operations are quite complex, occur in difficult political and social environments, and involve a number of tasks and subtasks, it is difficult, if not impossible, to write specifications concerning the procedures for each. Even if that could be done, very few contractors would agree to such provisions precisely because that sort of contract might limit innovation and efficiency—and ultimately profit. One could argue that the more restrictive the specifications written into a contract, the more expensive (and less cost efficient) the contract will become as the contractor seeks to protect his profit margin. It should be noted, however, that one potentially effective mechanism to control contractor performance was used in Bosnia: contract employees working with UNPROFOR in transportation and communications are under the direct supervision of the UNPROFOR staff, which can presumably oversee their actions and hold them accountable.[15] Although the record is incomplete, it appears that this system was at least somewhat effective.

Thus, contracting is disadvantageous when "means matter" because by contracting out, the government typically loses some control over *how* the tasks are accomplished. When accountability for and control of every action is critical, outsourcing can pose problems, especially when sensitive decisions affecting or defining U.S. policy are at stake.[16] This is particularly important when the activities of the contractor are likely to have a bearing on the ability of the government to accomplish its overall objectives in peace operations. In such cases, the way a contractor performs can either reinforce the positive attributes of the operation and enhance local consent—or undermine it. For example, contractors often rely on local labor pools to perform tasks under contract. However, if the contractor makes an error and hires the wrong segments of the local population, then a politically tense situation may be exacerbated. If, for instance, the peace operation involves reducing tensions between two different ethnic groups, the hiring of laborers from one group in disproportionate numbers by a contractor may be seen as an indication that the force is no longer impartial. An even more direct example where lack of effective control can have an adverse impact may be found in the performance of tasks relating to law and order. In such cases, strict control of the actions of public safety forces may be important for gaining the confidence and consent of the local population. Under these circumstances, accountability and control of every aspect of performance are crucial and poor performance could impair U.S. goals. In such circumstances, decisionmakers may conclude that the risk of poor performance is less and control measures are more responsive if the public safety tasks are performed by military police rather than by a contractor.

Also, contracting out is problematic where there must be the capability to respond rapidly to unpredictable changes in the situation, because the government's ability to control the speed of the response is limited. As noted, if changes occur in the work requirements—whether as a result of changes in the operational environment or because of poorly written contracts—they will almost inevitably lead to expensive modifications of the contract that may more than offset potential savings.[17] Unlike governmental employees who theoretically can be ordered to perform new tasks almost immediately, contractors can fall back on the terms of the contract and thereby delay a response until adjustments are made in the contract. Thus, where the situation is dynamic and timely response to change is required, contracting may not contribute to effective overall performance.

On the other hand, one must bear in mind that, for some functions, contractors may have capabilities that extend beyond those of the government. For example, although it took several weeks for contracted water purification equipment to arrive in Rwanda, once the contractor assumed the water purification function, daily production more than doubled, which the government could not have done using its available resources. In such cases the government may be required to relinquish control if it wants increased capacity. In analyzing whether contractors might be useful during peace operations, planners must decide whether the increased capacity that contractors bring to an operation and the consequent conservation of government resources are worth the loss of control contracting may involve.

In addition, there are situations where "means matter" for political reasons. Contracting may have politically symbolic costs if it is perceived that the United States or the United Nations is unwilling to dedicate itself directly to the work.[18] One example might be if the United Nations contracted with private firms to maintain security in potentially explosive refugee camps under UNHCR administration (such as those for Rwandan refugees). This action sends a political message to the host government, the camp residents, and to others that the United Nations is unable or unwilling to do the work itself, which may in turn make more difficult the maintenance of camp security. Contracting may be interpreted as a sign of weakness or vulnerability by some; others may see contracting as a way of indicating that the force considers some aspect of the operations to be of too low a priority to merit professional attention. Either interpretation is likely to encourage potentially disruptive actors to take advantage of the situation.

On the other hand, if contracting requirements are pursued imaginatively, contractors may do much to assist in accomplishing overall objectives. If civilian workers are hired in ways that are acceptable to the local social and political structures, then contracting contributes to the well being of the population by providing a source of jobs and income. This, in turn, gives the population a stake in the continuing success of the operation, for as long as it continues without disruption, jobs are likely to continue also.

A final political-legal concern involves gaining permission as needed from host governments (or factions) for U.S. contractors to operate on their soil, and ensuring that the contract stipulates the conditions on which that permission is predicated. Gaining the requisite approval from foreign governments is certain to require the expenditure of political capital to get what some governments will view as special treatment for contractors. If the government fails to gain this permission, it may be sued by the contractors for not doing so. Once permission is granted, contracts that are especially clear as to the legal status, legal responsibilities, and privileges and immunities (or lack thereof) of the contractor are required. In some circumstances, drafting the contract may require participation by host governments at some level.

Permission or license to operate in foreign territories interjects yet another control requirement. U.S. contracting officers and performance supervisors must ensure that contractors adhere to the terms required by host governments in return for operating privileges. Failure to do so may damage U.S. efforts politically and, in extreme circumstances, may result in loss of vital capacities if a contractors operating privileges are suspended.

Conclusion

This discussion has outlined broad overlapping and interrelated categories of considerations for determining the costs and benefits of contracting for tasks during peace operations. Precisely defining the costs and benefits associated with contracting for performance of a specific task requires the study of issues related not only to cost savings, but also policy questions as well. Such questions include:

• The long- and short-term impact upon governmental capacity

• The importance of urgent or on-time performance to the accomplishment of mission objectives

• The degree of control that may be needed on the manner of performance versus the end product

• The likelihood that there will be changes in the operation that will require rapid response

• The symbolic importance of governmental performance

Outsourcing has played a beneficial role in a number of peace operations and should be considered as an option in the future so that military forces can concentrate on core competencies. Just as with contracting in other defense related situations, the costs and benefits for peace operations activities must be carefully scrutinized in advance to ensure that the unique requirements of peace operations are properly considered. Unless operational and support considerations are integrated into the process, the benefits of outsourcing may not be all that is desired.

Notes

1. See chapter 3 of *Directions for Defense: Report of The Commission on the Roles and Missions of the Armed Forces* for a discussion of other outsourcing and privatization issues.

2. Interviews of Ambassador Thomas Boyatt, President, United States Defense Systems, Inc. (USDS), Washington, DC, November December 1994.

3. There may be requirements or activities associated with peace operations for which the government lacks capabilities that are available to private contractors. For example, restoring and operating a railway system or performing functions associated with municipal governments. There may also be cases where the government cannot perform a particular function because another operation has a higher priority and has siphoned off the necessary resources.

4. John J. Donahue, *The Privatization Decision: Public Ends and Private Means* (New York: Basic Books, 1989), 79-98. Donahue sets out criteria for determining activities which the government should carry

out versus those appropriate for contracting.

5.   Private contractors have been employed for land mine removal in both Cambodia and Kuwait.

6.   Randall Schriver, (Commission staff), Memorandum on Privatization/ Contracting of Government Functions, Nov. 27, 1994.

7.   Telephone interview of Dept. of State officials, Office of Diplomatic Security, Washington, DC, December 1994.

8.   Ibid.

9.   Donahue, 90; Schriver memo.

10.   Donahue, 79, 165.

11.   Donahue, 107-109.

12.   Donahue, 80.

13.   Schriver Memorandum, 1.

14.   See Philip E. Fixler, Jr., and Robert W. Poole, "Can Police Services Be Privatized?" *Annals of the American Academy of Political and Social Science* 498 (July 1988): 108-18, for further discussion of this subject.

15.   Interview of Ambassador Boyatt, USDS.

16.   John D. Hanrahan, *Government by Contract* (New York: Norton, 1983), 89.

17.   Donahue, 79-80; Hanrahan, 89.

18.   Donahue, 156.

9. COALITION MANAGEMENT IN PEACE OPERATIONS

Antonia Handler Chayes and **Wendy J. Jordan**

The post-Cold War environment requires a shift in the ways the United States thinks about and prepares for the military operations of the future. One aspect of this shift is the emphasis on regional (rather than global) crises, not only in terms of fighting and winning, but also through a broader range of options including preventive peace operations. Whatever the response, it is likely to take the form of a coalition effort. Further, given the likelihood of even more unpredictable crises and contingencies in the years ahead, coalitions may not necessarily correspond to any of our existing alliances (e.g., NATO). They may be much more ad hoc and lack the carefully developed procedures that formal coalitions can count on to enhance interoperability.

While the National Security Strategy, the National Military Strategy, and various other documents indicate that the United

---

Dr. Antonia Chayes was a Commissioner on the CORM. She is a former Under Secretary of the Air Force and is currently the Co-Director of the Project on International Compliance and Dispute Resolution, Program on Negotiation, Harvard Law School. She is the author of numerous books and articles.

Wendy J. Jordan is a member of the CORM's professional staff. She was the chief of the Commission's study of coalition interoperability. Ms. Jordan previously served as a staff member in the U.S. House of Representatives.

States will always retain the ability to act unilaterally, they also indicate that it will seek to form coalitions to deal with complex problems, both to acquire additional assets (thus limiting the strain on U.S. forces and resources) and to generate broad legitimacy. The United States is less likely to act alone, unless a clear national interest is at risk, if it is possible to enlist the resources of other powers, including forces, weapons, and funding.[1] This chapter explores the considerations that have led the United States to plan to operate as part of a coalition, the extent to which existing international organizations can help in creating a coalition, and ways to improve coalition interoperability.

Why Coalitions?

Coalition operations are not easy to create or make work effectively. Accounts of coalition military operations are fraught with tales of tensions, compromises, and frequently dysfunctional arrangements that seem harder to manage than they are worth. More recently, the difficulties in Somalia and Bosnia have illuminated such tensions. Not only do contributing nations bring different capabilities and doctrinal approaches but also may have differing objectives and priorities.

As the United States discovered during the Gulf War, coalitions require extraordinary management skills and attention to maintain necessary military effectiveness and communication at all levels. This is especially true of ad hoc arrangements that lack the discipline and experience of long-term alliances, which, despite years of combined operations, can still experience difficulties. Even NATO, an alliance that has more than 40 years' experience in operating as a coalition, has faced tensions among members concerning the former Yugoslavia, although the differences are more in the broader arena of policy choices than over operational methods.

Given the fact that the United States has robust military capabilities in every mission area, should it bother with coalitions? Yes, for two important reasons. Most important, coalitions provide a certain amount of political viability and legitimacy. Second, coalitions may help defray operational costs that might become domestically unacceptable.

The legitimacy of coalition actions becomes very important in the post-Cold War era, particularly as the norms of appropriate intervention are more difficult to establish. Broad participation by nations in a coalition works more effectively to isolate opponents politically and economically. The isolation of Iraq involved a coalition that included a number of Iraq's trading partners that had long-term economically beneficial ties. The coalition occurred because of the egregious nature of Iraq's invasion of Kuwait, but built pressures of its own. Even nations outside the coalition were loath to provide support to Iraq in the face of such massive condemnation.

The very need for consensus that a coalition implies may be at once a source of tensions among its members and the glue that holds it together. Although it takes time and considerable diplomatic skill to craft objectives, once objectives are promulgated, it becomes difficult for those who approved them to renege on their commitments. On another level, consensus may make it easier to explain operations to—and maintain necessary support from—constituents.

International involvement in a coalition by neighbors in the region directly affected by the problem, is another important issue. On the negative side, it may emphasize old battlelines, yet such involvement may be crucial to the legitimacy of the intervention. With U.S. or Russian participation, it may be necessary to overcome perceptions of imperialism, which would upset the delicate balance that must be maintained for peace operations to succeed.

Conversely, if the United States works within a coalition it may help defuse domestic critics who argue against an overreliance on the United States as the world's policeman. The recent swell in isolationist rhetoric among American politicians has struck a responsive chord with the voters, whose economic and other domestic concerns are running high. American views run the gamut from any foreign assistance be a low budget priority to more conspiratorial extremist fears about U.N. world domination. Coalitions do not cure the post-Cold War popular concerns about appropriate U.S. involvement in crises throughout the world, but they do demonstrate a convergence of interest that may be persuasive in some crisis situations.

One element of coalition commitment of great importance to Americans is cost sharing, as achieved during the Gulf War. Clearly, if the cost of a peace operation can be shared with other nations and is not a heavy burden on the United States, it may be possible to ameliorate one level of political opposition. The expense of military operations may become a political tool by which the Congress can constrain the President's foreign policy. Congress, with the power of the purse[2] can truncate or end a peace operation. However, critics in Congress may be muted by coalition contributions.

More sensitive is the willingness of other nations to provide forces to augment or replace those of the United States, as some nations have done in Somalia and Haiti. It is axiomatic that the United States has some unique capabilities for large peace operations. Its logistics, communications, air superiority, and strategic transportation assets cannot be duplicated by any other nation. However, the bulk of the ground forces does not have to be from the United States. There is no reason why light infantry, military police, medics, truck drivers and a host of other skills cannot be provided by other nations, assuming they are properly trained and equipped. Such commitments reduce OPTEMPO and PERSTEMPO[3] issues and spread major risk—a telling point in the domestic U.S. political debate.

Commitment of these forces means that similar U.S. formations are not needed, but use of coalition forces is not an unmixed blessing. Depending on their ability to achieve interoperability with U.S. command and communications systems, and the amount of required support in a number of areas, coalition forces may still be a drain on resources. For example, if the forces offered by coalition partners are ill trained, then the United States might have to establish extensive programs to ensure that these forces are capable of performing their missions without undermining strategic goals and objectives through inappropriate actions. In other cases, even with long-time allies, including some NATO partners, sufficient quantities of interoperable communications systems are not available, requiring the United States to divert that equipment from reserve stocks or from other operations. Even forces that are adequately trained and able to communicate effectively may have little capability to provide their own logistical support within the framework of the U.S. logistics system. If coalition forces are to operate effectively in peace operations—or any other type of operation—such considerations should be addressed in advance and a requirements survey initiated across the range of potential coalition partners to ensure requirements are appropriately addressed in advance.

Coalition Partners and Coalition Operations

A core group of nations shares many of the same objectives and values with the United States and may contribute troops to peace operations in which the United States may also have an interest. Many of these nations (including Great Britain, Canada, France and Belgium, *inter alia)* are our NATO allies with whom we already enjoy a high degree of interoperability. These nations, and perhaps others, do not pose the same magnitude of problems for effective coalition operations as do nonalliance forces. Long-standing alliance agreements, joint training and exercise programs, and foreign military sales have helped produce this interoperability. However, NATO cannot now assume a lead role in peace operations throughout the world. Participation in an operation outside the NATO Area of Responsibility (AOR) involves a number of legal and political obstacles. Its charter is limited geographically, and its consensus rule of decisionmaking is a further constraint.

Member options also pose additional restrictions. Germany for example, has constitutional limitations on its ability to operate outside its borders. Several other NATO countries have restrictions on deploying conscripts, who constitute the bulk of their armed forces, outside their borders. Others have reduced their time of conscription to a year or less, barely enough time for basic military training, much less extensive overseas operational deployments. Moreover, NATO enlargement would impair interoperability and effectiveness for many years to come, even though participation could lend legitimacy in some crises. All these considerations contribute to the complexity of putting together widespread coalitions that rely on NATO effectiveness and experience for peace operations of long duration. Although initiatives for standardizing the planning and operating procedures for non-NATO members outside traditional AORs are underway, it may be difficult to make the NATO model applicable universally.

To the extent that peace operations are under UN auspices, it is likely that coalitions will include non-NATO members as well. In most regional crises outside NATO's AOR, legitimacy probably dictates the inclusion of some non-NATO nations with whom NATO nations have not exercised and with whom they lack interoperability. While it is difficult to foresee all potential coalition partners in advance, as plans for contingency operations unfold in accordance with various scenarios, it seems advisable to take at least a rough inventory of potential coalition members. This inventory should include a listing of capabilities and an estimate of the requirements for U.S. support during peace operations. As part of this process, planners should consider ways to deal with common problems and challenges.

The challenges of coalition operations are always formidable. They are even more so when dealing with a diverse coalition, one that might mix NATO nations, non-NATO nations that are militarily robust and participate at least occasionally in combined exercises with U.S. forces, and ill-equipped forces that have had little or no contact with U.S. or NATO forces. Perhaps the first challenge, both literally and figuratively, is how to communicate with one another. Coalition operations depend heavily on the ability to communicate, and success may depend on how well that is done. The rudimentary aspect of command, control and communications (C^3) systems and inadequacies in coalition-wide Identify Friend or Foe (IFF) systems, to cite just two examples, were difficult problems to overcome in the Gulf War.

The communications problem is complex and operates on at least three levels:

- First, the basic language barrier must be overcome. This is no small task, even in NATO where many officers are multilingual. In peace operations it looms larger because coalition participants must be able to communicate both among each other and with local inhabitants.[4] Often, military-to-military communications will occur at a much lower level than was the norm in Cold War NATO procedures when, as a rule, most interaction occurred at battalion and higher. Thus, a premium will be placed on acquiring sufficient linguists to prevent disruptions and tensions as a result of misinterpretations.

- The second level of the communications challenge involves the more subtle language differences and nuances occasioned by each nation's military culture. Although the same terms (i.e., attack, defend, secure, cordon) have a general meaning across nations, specific operational meanings differ. Accurate translation of a particular word is only part of the solution. The other part is conveying the specific meaning of terms and doctrinal connotations across military cultural lines.

- Communications are also hampered by equipment interoperability, the third level of the problem. In peace operations, as in conventional warfare, most intra-coalition communications at the tactical level will occur over radio nets. Until relatively recently, the U.S. Armed Forces had difficulty talking with each other in this manner. Thus, it should come as no great surprise that the potential exists for substantial problems among coalition partners. Sometimes this can be offset by assigning liaison teams to coalition formations as was done during the Gulf War. These teams, equipped with U.S. radios and partially manned by linguists, acted as go-betweens for various U.S. headquarters working with non-U.S. coalition forces. The solution worked reasonably well for the United States, although there were still problems caused by cultural misinterpretations. However, it required considerable manpower resources and a great deal of equipment. And, if a non-U.S. coalition member wished to speak with another non-U.S. coalition member directly, that problem was more difficult to resolve. Because communication is of critical importance during peace operations, equipment interoperability cannot be taken lightly.

Another major challenge is logistics support. Almost all armed forces have some ability to support themselves during operations[5]. However, the logistics of many nations is often tied into the national infrastructure. Because many potential coalition partners never intended their forces to operate beyond their borders—or at least not beyond the reach of the national infrastructure—operations at great distances can pose tremendous difficulties. The United States will frequently have to provide solutions if the coalition is to function effectively. There are also at least two levels to that problem:

• First, transportation to the AOR and within it can be beyond the means of many nations. Few states possess the strategic lift capabilities of the United States, but most countries will require some strategic lift to reach the AOR. In all likelihood, the U.S. will either have to provide this lift or make it available through contracting arrangements, as the Gulf War made clear. A substantial number of countries offered their services but relied on the United States to move their forces to the theater during that crisis. Transportation within the AOR can also present problems, especially when large quantities of supplies or large numbers of troops must be moved repeatedly over long distances. Nations whose presence is valuable for operational success may be dysfunctional once in the AOR simply because their organic transportation resources are too limited to provide the proper operational latitude.

● A second facet of the problem involves materiel support provided by the United States to coalition partners. Planners must assume that some materiel will have to be provided by the United States to some coalition participants and adjust logistics stockpiles accordingly. Even a few of the more capable coalition partners may need to rely on the United States temporarily until their own bases are up and running. In the worst case, guarantees of U.S. logistics support may be the *quid pro quo* for the operational support of other nations in peace operations. Whatever the case, the United States increased costs and resource expenditures over and above those for U.S. forces operating alone as part of the price for coalition operations[6].

A brief look at coalition participation in one peace operation illustrates some of these problems. Operation *Provide Comfort* (aid to Kurds in northern Iraq) was scheduled to last 11 days, but it is still ongoing more than 4 years later. Much of the logistics support still comes from the United States. Many national contingents arrived in northern Iraq without adequate prior coordination, with widely divergent capabilities for logistics support and with only a vague idea of how to acquire such support from the United States. In some cases, such basic items as tents and engineering and construction support, required in order to sustain operations, were provided by U.S. forces, who had not planned or programmed for these requirements.

Current Programs That Ease Interoperability Problems

Despite the difficulties of coalition operations, the United States already has taken a number of steps to enhance coalition effectiveness. There currently exist well-defined security

161

assistance programs that promote interoperability with our allies and potential partners, and, although they are not specifically crafted for a particular coalition or contingency, they serve to increase both capability and interoperability (assuming former allies do not become adversaries). For example, the Administration's FY96 budget request for various security assistance programs includes $100 million to support Partnership for Peace (PFP) activities, $5 million to assist in equipping the Baltic Peacekeeping Battalion and $20 million across seven Central European countries to improve defense infrastructure in order to facilitate interoperability with NATO. There are other programs as well that may, with some modification, help improve coalition interoperability for peace operations.

The Foreign Military Sales (FMS) program is perhaps the most longstanding example of ongoing security assistance programs. Allies and partners that purchase U.S.-made military equipment receive training that often includes an introduction to U.S. doctrine governing the equipment's use. Providing the equipment, the training, and an overview of U.S. doctrine are all important steps in achieving interoperability . However, partly because many of our allies are reducing defense spending at a rapid rate, FMS sales are expected to level off at slightly below $10 billion in the out-years, down from an all-time high of $33 billion in FY93. While these reductions may be in order, it is important to ensure that the rules that govern who receives the remaining resources include those nations that will be helpful in peace operations as well as in conventional warfare.

The Foreign Military Financing (FMF) program, a combination of U.S. government grants and loans, finance some existing security assistance programs. Although the funds are authorized and appropriated through annual Foreign Operations legislation, the program is executed by the Department of Defense. Annually, the vast majority — $3.1 billion — of the FMF account is earmarked for Israel and Egypt. In FY93 the total account was slightly more than $4.1 billion, with the remaining $1 billion going mainly for FMF loans to European countries. FY94 total funding dropped to just over $3.9 billion, with most of the residual $800 million again dedicated to European loans. FY95 funding was $3.77 billion. These expenditures are worthwhile, but it may be prudent to try to broaden FMF and include specific provisions in the program that require improving capabilities for interoperability during peace operations.

The International Military Education and Training (IMET) program is a system of grants offering professional military education (PME) courses to more than 2,000 foreign military and civilian personnel from over 100 countries annually. IMET is one of the programs most frequently mentioned by both U.S. and foreign officials when they are discussing the promotion of interoperability. Training of the military professionals of other countries is our most effective method of introducing them to U.S. doctrine, procedures, and equipment. The courses are offered in the United States at Service schools and colleges and in other countries by traveling training teams. Previously focused on respect for human rights, democratic institutions, and civilian control of the military, the IMET program has expanded to meet new demands from transitional democracies in the former Soviet Union, Africa, and Latin America. The expanded program includes defense resource management, military justice, and civil-military relations. FY94 funding was $22.25 million, while FY95 funding was $25.5 million. A greater investment might pay handsome dividends.

The Military-to-Military Contact Program (MMCP) is a recent initiative to provide a means of establishing contacts with the professional military establishments of emerging democracies in ECE and FSU nations. MMCP is facilitated by Military Liaison Teams that establish contacts within a country's defense ministry to identify needs associated with the rebuilding of the defense infrastructure in that country. The liaison team then creates a Traveling Contact Team with the necessary expertise. Other MMCP initiatives include familiarization tours, military conferences, and civilian and military exchange programs. Originally funded from regional Unified Command initiative funds, and privately through grants, this program has been widely hailed as a success story.[7]

Options for Improving Coalition Management in Peace Operations

If the largest problems facing a coalition are communications and logistics, what can be done, particularly within existing alliances and partnerships, to ameliorate those problems? Within NATO these challenges have been addressed for 45 years with continuing improvement. One option that is sometimes offered by way of solving some of these problems involves the prepositioning of stocks in NATO. If NATO as an organization were to be used repeatedly in peace operations, it might make sense to do a certain amount of prepositioning. However, since the United States has been involved in operations with *ad hoc* coalitions in areas as dispersed as Somalia and Haiti, prepositioning in Western Europe would be hard to justify. Some supplies to support the exercises of Partnership for Peace nations could be provided, however, to improve interoperability. Yet, if prepositioning is of questionable value at present, planning is not. On the assumption that NATO alliance members may work together in peace operations, as NATO or as an ad hoc coalition, planning becomes important and perhaps the planning process, which requires a great deal of coordination and discussion, is more important than the actual plan. During the process, responsibilities should be agreed to in advance so that potential partners understand what will be provided under what circumstances.[8]

If direct U.S. funding of such agreements is not politically feasible, the old NATO infrastructure fund, recently renamed the Security Investment Program, is a possible source of funding for the most basic supplies necessary when troops are operating in a multinational coalition. However, political considerations have made it extremely difficult to tap these funds in advance, and they would not be available to purchase materiel for non-NATO operations, even if the largest contributors to those operations were NATO members. Additionally, purchasing and titling matériel with these funds through the United Nations to support an UN-authorized operation could raise issues of control, as in Bosnia, and amount of contribution if normal UN assessment rates are used.

In any case, it is unlikely that many peace operations would involve only NATO members. A potential source of coalition partners is to be found among members of the Partnership for Peace (PFP) program. They are eager to join NATO and may be likely to join a coalition because they may view it as a training exercise or "tryout" for eventual NATO membership. Some training and experience with equipment can be especially useful for PFP nations that fall into this category. However, because of the previous status of most as members of the FSU or its client states, these nations have been ineligible for security assistance programs until very recently; some are still not eligible. Accordingly, little Westernmade hardware is in their inventories. These and other non-traditional partners are good candidates for increased participation in existing security assistance programs for the sale and granting of U.S. military equipment and accompanying training. But in these cases training becomes especially important. Simply handing complex communications equipment over to forces of a nation unfamiliar with U.S. or NATO systems will not go far toward making the coalition work. A PFP goal now is doctrinal and operational interoperability reinforced by combined exercises and the use of Western equipment.

The importance of combined exercises to promote interoperability with non-traditional partners is clear. However, distinctions must be drawn according to the military sophistication of the partner and exercises must be tailored to that level of sophistication. One can cite the success of the UNITAS series of exercises and the substantial progress made by the navies of Latin America in cooperation with the United States Navy as indicative of the value of combined exercises with nations of roughly the same capabilities as PFP nations.[9] European Command (EUCOM) has begun a schedule of combined exercises in which each of the services will interact with PFP nations.[10] One of the first was BREEZE 94, a combined maritime exercise with Bulgaria, Georgia, Ukraine, Greece, Turkey, and Russia.[11] In these first steps, the focus is likely to be on basic military cooperation rather than on complex operations. However, exercises such as these offer a marked increase in understanding and cooperation at the command level. Combining exercises with increased security assistance efforts is likely to increase the return on the investment of effort. In particular, it is possible to increase interoperability by increasing the exposure of these countries to the basics of IMET and MMCP. The less permanent versions of overseas presence—passing exercises, port visits, and the like— could help by encouraging command-level interaction between the countries.

Likewise, coalition support teams, using the U. S. Special Operations Command and Army Foreign Area Officer as models, with personnel trained specifically in the language, culture, and military culture of the partner could go far in increasing interoperability with non-traditional partners by working to overcome the existing language barriers. As stated earlier, these barriers do not begin and end with the national language spoken by a given country; they extend to the "military" language and training of the PFP and other nontraditional partners.

Where Does the United Nations Fit in the Picture?

At this writing, relations between the United Nations and NATO have become quite strained over control of NATO military operations in Bosnia. Yet it is likely that most peace operations involving the use of armed forces will continue to operate under some form of U.N. auspices where the U.S. and its NATO allies have great influence over decisions made in the Security Council. A good deal of disagreement over Bosnia has in fact been differing policy approaches among the Permanent-5. In fact, partly in recognition of this fact, the Secretary General has shown increasing flexibility with respect to the discretion accorded military commanders in mid-1995. Bosnia has been a crucible for the United Nations and has tested the capabilities beyond all previous limits. Its successes and failures must be considered in the light of other efforts to organize and manage coalitions from Cyprus to Cambodia.

For reasons of politics and legitimation, any U.N. coalition is likely to be ad hoc, to a certain extent—put together in light of the particular conflict it is designed to prevent or mitigate. Nonetheless, U.N. planners are aware of steps that it could take to strengthen a coalition and make it more immediately effective. Partly in response to earlier problems, the Secretary General of the United Nations began a new program, in late 1994, to enhance the short-notice deployability of U.N. forces and improve the planning and execution of operations. This initiative, the Standby Arrangements, is worth examining, if only because it offers an additional method to improve successful coalition operations.

The Arrangements are bilateral agreements, negotiated between the United Nations and individual member states to identify specific units and resources that *might* be available for peace operations, subject to further consultation. These assets could be made available to deploy within a specific period (defined as 7 to 30 days for UN peace keeping operations, depending on the unit's mission). However, call up authority does not rest with the Secretary General and deployment of these forces is not automatic. It is important to note that, once the Secretary General requests the force, the member state has the right to exercise its own, unique, internal approval process prior to actually deploying the unit.[12] In some countries, this approval process may be so lengthy as to negate the ability of the Secretary General to respond with any speed—or the country may decline to deploy the force at all.

Nonetheless, predesignation of resources is an interesting experiment. In theory, the Standby Arrangements will make it easier to construct and manage coalition operations. It is useful to have an inventory of the types of force packages that might be available as early as possible in the Security Council decision making process. Such knowledge lends an air of reality to the debate over mandates, objectives, and options, a crucial element for operational success as discussed in chapter 3. Also, knowing the size and location of units to be deployed facilitates transportation planning. However, since there is no mechanism to hold a state to its initial agreements, an inventory of available units may not translate into deployed units.

In addition, the Secretary General has realized, in part through the Bosnian experience, that it is difficult and probably damaging for the UN to engage in "peace enforcement", which is tantamount to war. There are situations in which such efforts are warranted or required, and can be justified under Chapter 7 of the U.N. Charter. Several nations, such as the United States in the Gulf and Haiti, can play the lead or even act as "subcontractor" to the United Nations. There is ample precedent for that. While Rwanda was not an enforcement operation, it might have become one, and France was accorded the lead there, as was Russia with respect to Georgia and the United States in Haiti. The United Nations does not have the resources, nor are nations willing to assume the risks and costs of the enforcement end of military peace operations without sufficient control of operational methods. For this reason, the lead nation concept, with international standards, may be a reasonable solution for now.[13]

Conclusion

There is little doubt that American domestic ambivalence about the value of coalitions will continue, as will the continuing need to work within them. Nor will it be possible to assure that for the foreseeable future, most coalitions will be adequately prepared and trained in advance to cope efficiently with the range of peace operations tasks they will face. The timing and location of crises remain unpredictable, and therefore the nature and composition of the response will necessarily be somewhat ad hoc.

However, recent experience has shown ways to improve coalition effectiveness, and many of these have been discussed in this chapter. As NATO evolves further, it can build upon the highly developed interoperability that is the result of nearly half a century of work. Partnership for Peace and its evolution will broaden that base. And even if the Alliance does not always act as NATO in peace operations, its members have formed the core forces for stressful peace operations, and can continue to do so, working together and drawing on the NATO experience.

The United States is unlikely to withdraw from the world, but it will not shoulder the costs and risks of quelling crises throughout it. This suggests a transformation of its leadership role that shifts a good deal of emphasis from crisis response to planning and preparation for the unexpected and unpredictable, while maintaining strength and readiness for those crises that might tax our military to the fullest.

Notes

1.   See *A National Security Strategy of Engagement and Enlargement* (Washington, DC: The White House, February 1995), and the *National Military Strategy of the United States: A Strategy of Flexible and Selective Engagement* (Washington, DC: The Joint Staff, February 1995).

2.   Article I, Section 9, Subsection 7, Constitution of the United States.

3.   OPTEMPO is the acronym for Operational Tempo or the rate at which forces are programmed to operate; PERSTEMPO, or Personnel Tempo, is a measure of the amount of time forces spend deployed away from their home garrisons.

4.   Communication requirements between coalition partners can be lessened somewhat if different nations are assigned discrete areas of operation. Even so, however, there will be a need for elements along the borders of these areas to communicate with adjacent units. See chapter 1 for a discussion of the interactions between peace operations forces and the local populations.

5.   Logistics includes supply, maintenance, services (such as decontamination, laundry and bath), transportation, and facilities. Doctrinally, it does not include medical support, although that is likely

to be a requirement, also.

6.   A third level involves logistics-related training requirements. Unlike the U.S. experience during the Cold War when logistics was considered to be a national responsibility exceptions to this rule were agreed to well in advance, there will be greater demands placed on U.S. logistics during coalition peace operations. These demands are likely to be of an ad hoc nature and come with little, if any, advanced warning. The U.S. logistics system is complex and it appears daunting to nations that operate in less demanding environments. Simply gaining access to matériel and services requires a certain amount of expertise, as does understanding the conditions for delivery and use.

7.   Department of Defense, Defense Security Assistance Agency (DSAA). Memorandum for Commission on Roles and Missions of the Armed Forces (Coalition Interoperability Team). November 30, 1994. MMCP was congressionally authorized as a free-standing program and funded at $12 million in FY95. Of this total, $10 million is for the European theater; the remaining $2 million is devoted to establishing contacts in the Pacific Command area of responsibility (AOR).

8.   There are other requirements as well, including access to satellite communications and intelligence data, which the United States should plan to provide to even our most robust NATO allies.

9.   Center for Naval Analyses, CQR 95-4, "Coalition Options for the Commission on Roles and Missions," March, 1995. This is a draft report that is subject to change with additional analysis.

10. Ibid.

11. Ibid, and Commander, Sixth Fleet. Memorandum for the Commission on Roles and Missions, "Preparation for Coalition Operation," dated March 7, 1995.

12. "United Nations Standby Arrangements System Description" and "The United Nations Standby Forces System (Briefing);" undated.

13. For a more detailed discussion, see Abram Chayes and Antonia Handler Chayes, eds. *Preventing Conflict in the Post-Communist World: Mobilizing International and Regional Organizations* (Washington, DC: Brookings Institute), forthcoming in autumn 1995.

APPENDIX:
Protocol for Peace Operations Case Studies

This protocol, published here as an aid to future case studies, provides a framework for examining case studies in a systematic way in order to ensure that all important military issues are addressed. Developed by Christine Cervenak and members of the CORM staff, it was used analyze a number of cases in order to identify key variables for success in peace operations. The protocol is generally couched in terms of questions, and the answers produced through analysis were often quite complex. The results of the case studies are summarized in Chapter 3 and reflected in other chapters throughout this work.

Overview

The protocol is divided into six parts:

1. A description of the context in which the operation occurs
2. A description of the objectives of the operation and the mandate that authorized the operation
3. Analysis of the degree of consent for the operation on the part of the belligerents and their supporters
4. Analysis of the degree to which the peace operations force maintained its impartiality and the effects thereof
5. Analysis of operational imperatives and issues in planning and execution
6. Assessment of the effectiveness of the operation.

Context for the Operation

Key factors include:

*   What is the historical setting for the conflict and the proximate causes?

- Who are the parties to the conflict and what are their interests and objectives?
- What efforts have been made by third parties to resolve the conflict prior to the peace operation? To what degree were they successful and why?
- At what point in the conflict was the peace operation established and at whose initiative? Was their involvement by the UN or other organizations?
- What was the rationale for initiating the operation? What assumptions were made concerning the operation when it was established?
- What political support did the operation receive from global and regional powers and what was the impact of that support? What type and degree of pressure did these powers exert on the antagonists?
- What was the relationship between the peace operation and larger, ongoing political efforts to resolve the conflict?

Mandate and Objectives

Description examines:

- What was the formal, legal mandate for the operation and how was it developed?
- If the mandate changed over time, why did such changes occur and how were they determined to be necessary?
- Did changes in mandates result in changes in the types of operations (e.g., peacekeeping to peace enforcement)? If so, what changes were made to force structures and capabilities?
- Where there political or other objectives that were not spelled out in the mandate?
- How were mandated and nonmandated political objectives translated into military objectives and specific tasks?
- Were military objectives clear and practicable, given the nature of the conflict and the available resources?
- Was there a match between political and military objectives?
- How was "success" defined and measured in terms of

accomplishing objectives? Did these measures change over the life of the mission?

• What was the relationship between military objectives (derived from the mandate) and other efforts to resolve the conflict? To what extent was military involvement necessary and useful in accomplishing those efforts?

Consent

Analysis includes:

• What was the level of consent for the peace operation on the part of all parties to the conflict and on the part of the non-belligerent portion of the population?

• If the level of consent changed over time, why did the change occur?

• Did the level of consent differ between the tactical, operational and strategic levels (i.e., was it supported by belligerent leadership but not by rank and file)?

• Did the level of consent vary for different operational activities (e.g., humanitarian assistance versus establishment of safe havens)?

• How was consent expressed by the population? Was it ever unclear that there was consent?

• How did operating forces deal with expressions of non-consent? Was the force tested by the belligerents to produce responses that might undermine consent?

• What dispute resolution mechanisms were developed?

• How did the consensual process work? To what extent was the military force required to enhance and maintain consent through mediation or negotiation?

• Which techniques, training, and equipment facilitated or hindered the consensual process?

• How did the level of consent affect the use of force?

• How did the level of consent influence the outcome of the operation?

Impartiality

Analysis includes:

- Were the forces impartial? Were they perceived by the parties to the conflict as impartial?
- To what extent did the perception of impartiality enhance or impede cooperation by parties to the conflict?
- What is the relationship between consent and impartiality?
- What actions influenced the perception of impartiality?

Operational Imperatives and Issues in Planning and Execution

Size, composition, levels of training and equipment of the force include:

- Which countries participated and what were their reasons for participating?
- Were there problems in recruiting nations to participate?
- Were there delays in providing forces after agreeing to do so? If so, with what effect on the operation?
- What was the size and composition of the force? Was it adequate given the operational objectives? How did composition and size change over time?
- What training specific to the operation was provided prior to deployment and during the operation? Who provided the training?
- How suitable was the training, and, if it was inadequate, what effect did this have on the operation?
- What types of equipment did the force have? Was equipment adequate and appropriate to the operational requirements and the physical environment?
- Were forces of different nations complementary or redundant?
- Were there discrepancies in levels of training and proficiency between national contingents?

- Were there discipline problems among troops engaged in peace operations?
- What level of interoperability between national contingents was achieved? How were problems overcome? What affect did this have on operational success?

Rules of Engagement (ROE) and Use of Force include:
- What were the ROE and how were they developed?
- Were ROE appropriate for the mandate and the military objectives?
- Was there a difference between the ROE as written and practiced?
- Did they change over time? If so what was the mechanism for changing them?
- If the type of peace operation changed, did ROE change appropriately?
- Were there violations of ROE? If so, with what consequences?
- Was force used during the operation? If so, with what effect on consent and impartiality? On the overall success of the operation?

Command, Control, Communications and Logistics include:
- What was the military command structure in the field? How was it related to the political/civilian control mechanisms?
- What difficulties were encountered in commanding and controlling multinational forces? Were special command architectures required?
- What problems existed in mechanisms to exchange information within the force? Between the force and local officials and parties to the conflict?
- Was intelligence shared? If so, how? What effect did intelligence sharing (or lack thereof) have on operational success?
- What was the relationship between military forces and private voluntary organizations and nongovernmental organizations? What mechanisms were in place to facilitate

coordination of effort?

- Were sufficient logistics assets available to the force? How were they provided and funded?
- Was local support available and how did it affect the operation?

Assessment of Operational Effectiveness

- Were the military objectives attainable at a reasonable cost with the assets available?
- How could the operation have been better organized and conducted?
- Which U.S. interests (if any) were affected by the operation and the way it was conducted?
- Which tasks could only have been performed by the military? Was it properly equipped and organized to perform them?
- Which tasks could only be performed by the U.S. military?
- Were there operational tasks performed by the military that might have been performed as well by non-military entities?
- What were the most commonly used items of equipment and technologies? What was the impact of them? If unavailable, what would the impact have been?
- How did the operation affect the readiness of U.S. forces? If the impact was adverse, how much time and expense was required to correct the deficiencies?
- If the U.S. was involved in the operation, what difference did that make? If the United States was not involved, would its involvement have made a difference?